TULLER CAFETERIA

COFFEE SHOP

CHECKER

CHECKER

CARS of the 1960s

BY THE AUTO EDITORS OF CONSUMER GUIDE®

Publications International, Ltd.

Louis Weber, CEO
Publications International, Ltd.
7373 North Cicero Avenue
Lincolnwood, Illinois 60712

Permission is never granted for commercial purposes.

ISBN-13: 978-1-4127-1391-7
ISBN-10: 1-4127-1391-9

Manufactured in China.

8 7 6 5 4 3 2 1

Credits

Photography:

The editors would like to thank the following people and organizations for supplying the photography that made this book possible. They are listed below, along with the page number(s) of their photos.

Mike Baker: 103, 167; **Roger D. Barnes:** 93; **Scott Baxter:** 152; **Ken Beebe:** 99, 165, 189; **Joe Bohovic:** 61; **Scott Brandt:** 177; **Michael Brown:** 100; **Chan Bush:** 67, 75, 134, 146, 153; **Gary L. Cook:** 92; **Dennis Doty:** 41; **Thomas Glatch:** 9, 11, 12, 13, 17, 19, 37, 39, 47, 57, 61, 68, 74, 82, 90, 94, 101, 123, 125, 128, 138, 149, 175, 183; **Mark Gordan:** 178; **Gary Greene:** 55, 59, 69, 93, 97, 119, 181, 189; **Sam Griffith:** 18, 27, 52, 60, 72, 84, 104, 124, 139, 145, 154, 156, 166, 168, 173, 178, 179, 182; **Mike Hastie:** 93; **Jerry Heasley:** 71, 76, 148, 162, 169; **John Heilig:** 167; **Don Heiny:** 13, 30, 35, 39, 40, 91, 113, 128, 139, 146, 153, 159, 180; **Alan Hewko:** 70, 75; **S. Scott Hutchinson:** 33; **Bud Juneau:** 36, 39, 52, 106, 114, 117, 121, 123, 131, 141, 160, 179, 185; **Milton Kieft:** 51, 58, 60, 78, 81, 82, 104, 108, 116, 147, 149, 150, 155, 174, 188; **Nick Komic:** 133, 162; **Howard Korn:** 93; **Lee Angle Photography:** 65; **Dan Lyons:** 58, 76, 95, 101, 112, 127, 156, 172, 184, 188, 189; **Vince Manocchi:** 20, 24, 26, 33, 34, 35, 37, 42, 45, 51, 54, 56, 61, 65, 66, 67, 75, 79, 80, 83, 87, 88, 89, 94, 95, 96, 98, 99, 103, 104, 105, 107, 110, 113, 118, 119, 120, 121, 122, 124, 126, 128, 129, 131, 132, 133, 134, 135, 136, 137, 139, 141, 142, 144, 147, 148, 150, 151, 157, 158, 161, 164, 165, 169, 174, 176, 180, 182, 183, 186, 187, 188, 190; **Mark McMahon:** 45; **Craig E. Middleton:** 89; **Doug Mitchel:** 29, 49, 51, 52, 54, 55, 59, 61, 70, 71, 73, 76, 77, 78, 81, 85, 86, 91, 97, 99, 103, 105, 108, 109, 112, 113, 117, 118, 120, 121, 125, 126, 127, 130, 137, 140, 145, 150, 151, 155, 156, 158, 159, 162, 166, 167, 169, 174, 184, 189, 198; **Ron Moorhead:** 183, 189; **Mike Mueller:** 11, 44, 47, 68, 70, 72, 73, 85, 114, 116, 140, 152, 155, 157, 168; **David Newhardt:** 33, 35, 103, 107, 111, 117, 118, 134; **Bob Nicholson:** 14, 16, 64, 122, 165, 174, 178; **Nina Padgett:** 45, 112, 113, 129; **Stephen Parezo:** 165; **Jay Peck:** 111; **Blake Praytor:** 34; **Chris Ranck:** 140, 152; **D. Randy Riggs:** 85; **Jeff Rose:** 69, 79, 82; **Tom Shaw:** 20, 79, 115, 170; **Gary Smith:** 30, 40, 43, 74, 96, 150, 164, 170, 179; **Robert Sorgatz:** 74; **Mike Spenner:** 62, 74; **Richard Spiegelman:** 184, 187, 190, 191; **Steve Statham:** 120; **Alex Steinberg:** 138; **Rick Stiller:** 85; **Tom Storm:** 30; **Richard Szczepanski:** 90; **David Talbot:** 38, 58; **David Temple:** 33, 46, 58, 62, 64, 67, 71, 72, 78, 84, 103, 106, 110, 136, 145, 149, 153, 159, 160; **Bob Tenney:** 48, 58, 77; **Phil Toy:** 35, 38, 41, 63, 87, 102, 130, 158, 169; **Paul Tuttle:** 160; **Rob Van Schaick:** 78, 108; **W.C. Waymack:** 8, 9, 10, 15, 16, 41, 42, 43, 44, 48, 50, 51, 52, 56, 59, 60, 62, 64, 65, 69, 74, 90, 94, 99, 101, 102, 105, 106, 109, 110, 111, 115, 118, 119, 123, 127, 132, 133, 136, 137, 143, 144, 148, 152, 155, 158, 160, 161, 162, 163, 164, 167, 170, 171, 173, 175, 177, 178, 179, 180, 183, 187, 188; **Nicky Wright:** 12, 23, 68, 75, 79, 92, 104, 114, 126, 140, 167, 186

Front Cover: Ron Kimball Photography
Back Cover: Milton Kieft; Vince Manocchi; Doug Mitchel; Bob Nicholson; David Temple
Title Page: Vince Manocchi

Owners:

Special thanks to the owners of the cars featured in this book for their cooperation.

Dale and Cindi Adams: 9; **Fred Ahern:** 16; **David Aiken:** 153; **Roy Alberson:** 110; **James Alexander:** 148; **James Allen:** 163; **Michael Allender:** 109; **A. Boyd Anderson:** 112; **Bill Anderson:** 160; **Donald Anderson:** 111; **Jim Anderson:** 148; **Robert Anderson:** 109; **Bill Andrews:** 79; **Dan Armstrong:** 103; **Jim Ashworth:** 117; **Louis Baiocco:** 134; **Howard Baker:** 149; **Jeffrey Baker:** 74; **D'Arcy Ballinger:** 113; **Ray Banuls:** 58; **John Baritel:** 161; **Bill Barnes:** 68; **Larry Barnett:** 58; **C.C. Barnette:** 160; **Joseph Barrera:** 96; **Dave Bartholomew:** 70, 75; **Carl Beck:** 121; **Robert Becker:** 113; **Robert Beesley:** 81; **John Begian:** 43; **Dennis Begley:** 114; **Jim Behrendt:** 150; **Bill and Kathy Berks:** 139; **Rod and Claudia Bjerke:** 97; **Melvin and Keitha Blackford:** 127; **Eugene and Sharon Blanc:** 118; **Doug and Linda Bolen:** 74; **Ken Boorsma:** 90; **Leon Bosquet:** 76; **Jim Bowersox:** 160; **William Bowker:** 67; **John Breda:** 104; **Dr. David George Briant:** 45; **Milt McMillen and Paul Brieske:** 37, 39, 123; **Steve Brocker:** 35, 38; **Frederick Brown:** 139; **Scott Brubaker:** 58; **E. Slocum and R. Brumbaugh:** 29; **Frank Burnham:** 20; **Bryan Burns:** 128; **David and Linda Burpeau:** 111; **Stephen Campbell:** 159; **Lawrence Camuso:** 41; **Kim Cardin:** 102; **Joe Carfagna:** 39; **Stephen Cargile:** 186; **Ken Carmack:** 23; **Richard Carpenter:** 33, 45, 161; **Donnie Carr:** 52; **Luis Chanes:** 118; **Stu Chapman:** 190; **John and Arlys Chesnutt:** 59; **Roger Clements:** 100; **Marilyn Cliff:** 180; **Harley Cluxton III:** 112; **Jerry Coffee:** 145; **Mick Cohen:** 18; **Larry Coleman:** 136; **Community Trading Center:** 58; **John Cook:** 120; **Steve and Andrea Cook:** 144; **Bill and Regina Cooley:** 187; **Dr. Randy and Freda Cooper:** 107, 151, 164; **Virgil Cooper:** 131; **Roger and Ann Copp:** 143; **Dennis and Cheri Coronado:** 133; **Donald Crile:** 174; **Thomas Crockett:** 174; **Ed Cunneen:** 179; **James Cunningham:** 33; **Dan Curry:** 76; **Custom Automotive Services:** 133; **John Danell:** 183; **Dan Darling:** 140; **Jim Davidson:** 132; **Chris Davis:** 52, 59; **Connie Davis:** 59; **Myron Davis:** 47; **Garry Day:** 119; **Chuck and Sutton Decker:** 188; **Alex Deeken:** 52; **Jack DeGroot:** 124; **David Dehaan:** 19; **Norman Deles:** 13; **Harry DeMenge:** 66; **John DeVed:** 95; **Keith Devereux:** 104; **Ed Dewitt:** 52; **John Diefenbach:** 132; **Rocky DiOrio:** 103; **Mason Dixon:** 79; **David Domash:** 95; **Robert Dowd:** 93; **Ralph Dowling:** 91; **Jeffrey Drucker:** 98; **John Duffek:** 57; **Keith Duncan:** 155; **Donald and Chris Dunn:** 116; **David Duthie:** 55; **Evan Eberlin:** 111; **Les Edwards:** 155; **Jim Egelhoff:** 187; **Roland Eggebrecht:** 183; **Jim Elijah:** 198; **Jim and Val Ellerbrock:** 105; **Fred Elliot:** 75; **Mike Elward:** 45; **Rob Embleton:** 168; **Howard Engerman:** 159; **Fred Engers:** 182; **James and Mary Engle:** 162; **Greg Englin:** 126; **Gil Espinosa:** 169; **Margaret Evans:** 162; **Phil Fair:** 44; **Clifford Fales:** 36; **Russel Farris:** 189; **Robert and Gene Fattore:** 124; **Eugene Fattore, Jr.:** 166; **Linn Fauke:** 8; **Jose and Marina Felix:** 136; **Joel Ferris:** 93; **Patricia Feutz:** 149; **Dave and Monica Finan:** 71; **William Finney III:** 51; **Jeanne Finster:** 161; **John and Mary Jean Flory:** 140, 152; **John Fobair:** 17; **Robert Forker:** 106; **Brad Frank:** 65; **Larry Frank:** 75; **Al Fraser:** 79; **David Freedman:** 188; **Anthony Freels:** 145; **David Freeman:** 70; **John Fuller:** 148; **Kevin Fuller:** 105; **Irene Galier:** 108; **Anthony Garcia:** 35; **Gil Garcia:** 63; **Paul Garlick:** 9; **Jerry Garvin:** 24; **Gregory Gates:** 99; **Brian Gatzow:** 90; **Paul and Julie Gelinis:** 87; **Tony and Suzanne George:** 68; **John and Jeanne Germine:** 137; **Jack Gersh:** 180; **Jerry and Louise Gibino:** 114; **Ben Gipson:** 39; **Dave and Mary Glass:** 156; **Chuck Goode:** 88; **Jerry Goodwin:** 155; **Larry Gordon:** 130; **Stephen Gottfried:** 187; **David Griebling:** 60; **Jack Gross:** 40; **Denny Guest:** 49; **Wanda Habenicht:** 145; **Harry and Donna Hadley:** 130; **Robert Hallada:** 141; **JoAnn Hammel:** 127; **Jerry Hammer:** 147; **Anthony Hanebrink:** 51; **David Harkey:** 83; **James Harris:** 106; **Garnet Harry:** 93; **Ralph Hartsock:** 52; **Robert Hassebroek:** 10; **Ken Havekost:** 12; **Jon Havens:** 177; **Stanley Haveriland:** 190; **Roy Hawkins:** 33; **Gregg and Nancy Hawley:** 165; **Ronald Hayden:** 90; **Joe Hayes:** 99; **Alan Hecht:** 64; **Chuck Henderson:** 137; **Scott Henderson:** 165; **Glenn Hickman:** 103; **Garth Higgins:** 122, 141; **Elizabeth Hilbrandt:** 184; **Joe and Lana Hill:** 84; **Larry Hills:** 129; **Russell Hoeksema:** 115; **Bill Hoff:** 169; **Rich Hogbin:** 182; **Tim Holsapple:** 107; **David Hooten:** 82; **Henry Hopkins:** 35; **Tony Hossain:** 162; **Lea and Bill Huetteman, Jr:** 158; **Jeff Hughes:** 150; **Derek Humphrey:** 121; **Henry Isaksen:** 138; **Michael Jackson:** 98; **Cherie Jacobson:** 103; **James and Ione Jander:** 167; **Anthony Johnson:** 134; **Ron Johnson:** 181; **Todd Johnson:** 170; **Albert Jones:** 152; **Bill Jones:** 131; **Nick Juliano:** 65; **Aaron Kahlenberg:** 61; **John Karaway:** 11; **Lee Keeney:** 102; **Dave and Cindy Keetch:** 144, 158; **Michael and Patricia Kelso:** 139; **Ron Kendall:** 153; **Royce and Clydette Kidd:** 67; **Robbie Kincaid:** 11; **Jon and Melanie King:** 74; **George Kling:** 126; **Michael Klyde:** 110; **David and Phyllis Knuth:** 116; **Mark and Ellen Koehler:** 93; **Scott Koeshall:** 101; **Larry Koetting:** 133; **William Kramer:** 61; **Jim Labertew:** 74; **William Lajeunesse:** 172; **Sandra Landry:** 107; **Mr. and Mrs. Terry Lange:** 134; **Matt Lazich:** 183; **Jim Lee:** 176; **Steve Nye and Ken Leighton:** 37; **Aivar Lejins:** 34, 35; **Doug LeMay:** 189; **Jack and Cheryl Lenhart:** 85; **Tony Leopardo:** 169; **Harold Lichty:** 188; **Charley Lillard:** 179; **Mark Lob:** 122; **James and Patricia Locher:** 178; **James and Robert Lojewski:** 27; **Douglas Lombardo:** 78; **Rob Long:** 107; **Phillip and Sandy LoPiccolo:** 142; **Terry Lucas:** 126; **Joseph and Suzanne Lysy:** 126; **Jim MacDonald:** 155; **Sean Machado:** 35; **John Machejewski:** 26; **Craig Macho:** 89; **Bob Macy:** 148, 162; **Garey Maib:** 113; **Larry Maisel:** 101, 109; **Donald and Janet Mallinson:** 164; **James and Sandy Marcellus:** 164, 170; **Junior Markin:** 152; **Larry Martin:** 41, 43, 44, 48, 132, 173, 175; **George Mason:** 34; **Ralph Mathiot:** 189; **Cliff Mathos:** 177; **Bob Mayer:** 86; **Brian McArthur:** 175; **Jade McCall:** 147; **Barry McCaw:** 189; **Gary McGee:** 56; **Bryan McGilvray:** 77; **Terry McGlasham:** 127; **Paul McGuire:** 168; **Garry McKinney:** 58; **Ken McMullen:** 179; **Charles McMullin:** 123; **Jeffrey Meier:** 94; **Lawrence Melton:** 9; **Michael Mennela:** 121; **Greg and Rhonda Meredyk:** 54; **Marty and Jacque Metzgar:** 169; **Alan Meyer:** 157; **Marty Meza:** 136; **Midwest Car Exchange, Inc:** 77; **Paul Miedema:** 69; **Harold Miller:** 171; **Harry and Carol Miller:** 167; **Larry and Karen Miller:** 165; **Norm and Judy Miller:** 158; **Greg Minor:** 139; **Amos Minter:** 48; **Connie and Larry Mitchell:** 174; **Frank Monhart III:** 104; **Trey Monroe:** 170; **Charles Montano:** 112; **Manny Montgomery:** 65; **Warren Moody:** 137; **Thomas Moore:** 111; **Earl Morgan:** 115; **Robert and Carole Morin:** 180; **Roger Moser:** 83; **Bob Mosher:** 51; **Dale Mueller:** 42; **Jim Mueller:** 85; **John and Pat Mueller:** 183; **Keith Mueller:** 152; **Vince Muniga:** 74; **Allan Murray:** 75; **Ed Musial:** 156; **Jon Myer:** 188; **Wesley Myrick:** 92; **Jason Mytar:** 146; **M. Randall Mytar:** 165; **Linda Naeger:** 181; **Barbara Nave:** 30; **Joan and Edward Neff:** 62; **Greg Nichols:** 34; **Jim Noel:** 138; **Barry Norman:** 94; **Donald Oehlert:** 170; **Ted Onufryk:** 128; **Jack and Lee Oulundsen:** 139; **Nicholas Pagani:** 128, 146; **Mr. and Mrs. Rob Paino:** 95; **Samuel Pampenella, Jr:** 114; **Anthony Patane:** 188; **Bonnie Patane:** 189; **Rudy and Bonnie Patane:** 184; **Bob Patrick:** 185; **Jim Patterson:** 169; **Rear Admiral Thomas J. Patterson:** 123; **Lawrence Pavia:** 60; **Thomas Payne:** 108; **Andre Pearson:** 158; **John Pegg:** 160; **Jim Perrault:** 82; **Joseph Pessetti:** 91; **Stan Peterson:** 92; **John Petras:** 108; **Sam Pierce:** 149; **Joe Pieroni:** 55; **Robert Pippins:** 14; **Charles Plylar:** 114; **Mr. and Mrs. Bob Polidan:** 40; **Michael Porto:** 42, 135; **Pro Team Corvette:** 125; **Jeff Quinn:** 62; **Stephen Quirolo:** 41; **Larry Raines:** 120; **Mark Raley:** 41; **Bruce Rambler:** 30; **Marie Rand:** 71; **M.G. Pinky Randall:** 179; **Roger Randolph:** 86; **Les Raye:** 147; **Dennis Reboletti:** 178; **Virgil Recker:** 101; **Danny Reed:** 149; **Chris Reuther:** 166; **Gilbert Reyes:** 145; **Mark Rice:** 119; **Fayegene and Rayma Rippelmeyer:** 60; **Dave Ritchie:** 129; **Jerry Robbin:** 85, 105; **Rick Roberts:** 178; **Dane Robinson:** 62; **Gary Robley:** 120; **Bob Roeper:** 80; **Keith Rohm:** 79; **Don Rook:** 72; **Nino Rosso:** 117; **Andy and Merlene Rueve:** 136; **Rod Ryan:** 125; **Carl Sable:** 46; **Darryl Salisbury:** 30; **Anthony Sanders:** 148, 161; **Rick Santelli:** 84; **Joe Saunders:** 73; **Mike and Jim Schaudek:** 158; **Tom Schay:** 142; **Gary Schneider:** 76; **Howard Schoen:** 172; **Mike Schowalter:** 96; **Bill Schrock:** 41; **Allen Schroer:** 69; **Paul Schult:** 61; **Lou Schultz, Jr:** 72; **Owen Schumacher:** 67; **Nick Schwartz:** 97; **Sam Scoles:** 89; **Doug Scott:** 134; **Robert Secondi:** 118; **Steven Senseson:** 109; **Owen Sessions:** 150; **Rob and Dottie Sharkey:** 98; **M.J. Shelton:** 184; **James Shiels:** 159; **Show 'N Tell Muscle Car:** 71; **JW and Barbara Silveira:** 106; **Duane Silvius:** 72; **Robert Simpson:** 64; **Glenn Skidmore:** 15; **Roy Sklarin:** 33; **Jack Sowchin:** 70; **Mike Spaziano:** 83; **Frank Spittle:** 46, 99; **Ron and Lyn Stauder:** 64; **Ralph Stegall:** 151; **Rick and Mary Steiner:** 163; **Elmer Sterthman:** 163; **Ron Stewart:** 56; **Charles Stinson:** 155; **Brian Stouck:** 190; **Kimberly Strauss:** 167; **Dale Street:** 42; **John Strewe:** 121; **Rick Stroh:** 119; **Nate Studer:** 68; **Tom and Nancy Stump:** 167; **George and Patricia Stumpe:** 50; **Larri Stumpf:** 35; **James Suther:** 170; **Joe Sutter:** 128; **Larry and Loretta Swedberg:** 174; **Steve Sydell:** 154; **Fred and Jan Sydral:** 178; **Brad and Bev Taffs:** 191; **Dick and Lance Tarnutzer:** 47; **David Temple:** 110; **Michael Tesauro, Jr:** 101; **Gary Thalman:** 78; **Keith Thompson:** 51; **Robert Thornton:** 186; **George and Tina Timm:** 115; **Michael Timothy:** 117; **James and Ellen Tremain:** 99; **Phil Trifaro:** 156; **Barry Troup:** 157; **Gary Tucker:** 62; **John Tucker:** 69; **Dennis Urban:** 150; **Jim and Cheryl Utrecht:** 155; **Larry and Sandra Van Horn:** 187; **Nick Vandewater:** 73; **Mike Venarde:** 118; **Steve Verderber:** 105; **John Vetter:** 94; **Joseph and Vallerie Volk:** 16; **Volo Auto Museum:** 78, 108; **John Wacha:** 140; **Linda Wade:** 97; **Larry and Beverly Wake:** 94; **Brent Walker:** 87; **Bruce Wanner:** 13; **Wayne and Terri Warner:** 108; **Alois Peter Warren II:** 38; **John and Connie Waugh:** 103; **Judge Lewis Weinstein:** 113; **George Weisser:** 81; **Charlie Wells:** 82; **Leo Welter:** 189; **Tom West:** 140; **Cheryl Samuel and Mike White:** 12; **Joyce and Jim Wickel:** 85; **Vanetta Wilkerson:** 120; **Randy and Jean Williams:** 145; **Sherman Williams:** 104; **Sam Wilson:** 103; **Blake Withrow:** 153; **Bill Woodman:** 173; **Janet Carter Wright:** 184; **Albert Yaccarino:** 128; **David Yordi:** 157; **George Young:** 54; **Rich and Joan Young:** 167; **Vince Zankich:** 88; **Robert Ziegler:** 20; **Charles Ziska:** 95

Special thanks to the photographic and media services groups of the following organizations:
Daimler-Chrysler, Ford Motor Company; General Motors Corporation

CONTENTS

FOREWORD

America went through enormous change in the 1960s, and the cars of the decade changed with it. A spirit of innovation ruled Detroit. The single-car model lines of the 1950s would no longer suffice. A fragmenting market demanded a broader range of choices, and automakers delivered.

They introduced compact cars and midsized models. A rebellious young generation was coming into its own, and Detroit tapped it too. The ponycar and muscle car were born, and the personal-luxury car attracted a wider audience than ever before. These fresh designs broke free of tradition, and reflected the decade's atmosphere of personal freedom.

These pages explore those new horizons, and celebrate the wonderous cars that help keep the spirit of the Sixties alive.

1969

With its fortuitous late-fifties emphasis on compact Ramblers, American Motors entered the Sixties a solid fourth in U.S. car sales. Under the direction of straitlaced CEO George Romney, AMC/Rambler had formed an image as a provider of prudent, economical compact cars—just what the buying public was looking for after the recession of 1958. Romney departed the company in 1962 to become governor of Michigan, and former sales manager Roy Abernethy stepped in.

Abernethy had ambitious plans to take on the Big Three in nearly every mass-market sector, and expanded AMC's product line accordingly. Astute restyling and savvy use of shared components allowed the company to offer a range of "new" products while minimizing tooling costs. The company's best products, such as the all-new-for-1963 Classics and Ambassadors, could stand toe-to-toe with GM, Ford, and Chrysler in terms of quality and innovation.

As the automotive marketplace became more youth- and performance-oriented, AMC's sensible-shoes image was seen as more of a liability than an asset. The company began to phase out the stodgy Rambler name in 1966, marketing its cars as "AMCs" instead. The ill-fated 1965 Marlin fastback was a misconceived attempt to capture the burgeoning "personal car" market, and disappeared after three years of disappointing sales. The aggressive product line expansion came up short as well, as AMC was overwhelmed by offerings from its larger, more established rivals. Sales sputtered: AMC lost a staggering $75.8 million for 1967, and Abernethy was replaced by former Ford man Bill Luneberg.

The company rebounded somewhat in 1968 with the introduction of the Javelin, a semifastback hardtop "ponycar" in the Ford Mustang image. The Rambler name was retired for good after 1969, but went out with a bang on the 1969 Hurst SC/Rambler, a junior muscle car with a whimsical personality.

The AMC name would move on into the Seventies with reasonable success, but, in the end, the company simply didn't have the resources to become a serious competitor in the mainstream automotive market. The firm gamely managed to hold on all the way through 1987, when America's last independent automaker vanished to become part of Chrysler Corporation.

1

1. The Rambler American line motored into the new decade with no fundamental changes, save the addition of a four-door-sedan body style. This is the $2059 Custom. 2. The compact car-market was expanding quickly in 1960, as the Big Three rushed new small cars into production. This brochure proclaimed the Rambler American "the most imitated car in America." 3. This American Custom two-door sedan is accessorized with fog lights, "half moon" headlight covers, and a continental kit. 4. Larger Ramblers were attractively restyled, gaining smoother lines, cleaner grilles, less-intrusive slope-backed windshield pillars, and new taillights. Exclusive to the top-line Ambassador series was the "Scena-Ramic" windshield, which was curved at the top as well as the sides. This Ambassador Custom four-door sedan wears Festival Rose and White two-tone paint. 5. The Rambler Six line came standard with a 127-horsepower inline six. A 138-hp version was optional. Pictured here is the $2383 Custom four-door sedan. 6. The Super Cross Country wagon came in six-passenger form with a drop-down tailgate (shown) or a new eight-passenger version with a side-opening rear door.

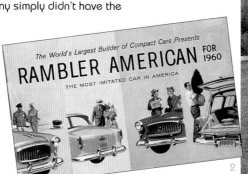

The World's Largest Builder of Compact Cars Presents

RAMBLER AMERICAN FOR 1960

THE MOST IMITATED CAR IN AMERICA

2

3

4

5

6

AMERICAN MOTORS

All New! A Convertible with Rambler Excellence

AMERICA'S NEWEST, SPORTIEST, LOWEST PRICED!

1. Americans were smartly reskinned for 1961, wearing boxy new sheetmetal over the existing chassis. The rounded styling of the 1958-60 American–itself a carryover from the earlier Nash Rambler–gave way to boxier contours with a flat hood and reshaped windshield, as on this Custom four-door sedan. **2.** American two-door wagons, like this Echo Green example, were outsold by the new-for-'61 four-door wagon body style. **3.** As before, the American model line ascended through DeLuxe, Super, and Custom models. The new-for-'61 convertible body style was exclusive to the

Custom series. At $2369, it was the most expensive American. DeLuxes and Supers were powered by a 195.6-cubic-inch "flathead" six that made 90 horsepower. Customs got a higher-compression overhead-valve version that made 125 hp. **4-5.** The spunky Metropolitan was powered by a 1500cc (or 90.9-cubic-inch) Austin 4-cylinder that made 55 hp. Sales of the British-built subcompact plummeted to a mere 969 units for '61.

IMPORTED

Metropolitan "1500"

"Luxury in Miniature"

6. *The 108-inch-wheelbase line was retagged Rambler Classic for 1961, as the Rebel moniker was temporarily dropped. A styling update included a lower hood and an eggcrate grille with integrated headlights.* 7. *Ambassadors got an unusual shovel-nose facelift with heavily hooded headlamps and a raked inverted-trapezoid grille. Buyers didn't seem to care for the new "European" styling, as Ambassador sales dropped 21 percent, to 18,842 units. Pictured here is the $2682 Custom four-door sedan. The Ambassador's 327-cubic-inch V-8 was rated at 250 horsepower with the standard two-barrel carburetor, or 270 hp with the optional four-barrel carb.* 8. *An Ambassador Custom six-passenger wagon started at $2986. Pillarless hardtop sedans and wagons were dropped from the Ambassador lineup for '61.*

SCORECARD 1961

MAKE	TOTAL PRODUCTION	MKT POSITION
AMBASSADOR	18,842 ▼	
AMERICAN	136,003 ▲	3rd ▲
CLASSIC	223,057 ▼	

AMERICAN MOTORS

1

2

3

New Style · New Savings
New Safety RAMBLER For 1962

1. *Ambassadors lost their distinctive styling and exclusive 117-inch wheelbase for 1962; they now rode the same 108-inch wheelbase as the Classic line. However, Classics no longer offered a V-8 option, making the Ambassador the only AMC car that came so equipped. That might explain why Ambassador output nearly doubled, to 36,171 units for the model year.* **2.** *Ambassadors wore unique side trim and square taillights in place of the Classics' round units. Both Ambassadors and Classics lost their vestigial fins.* **3.** *The Classic line's inline six-cylinder came in 127-horsepower or 138-hp forms. Pictured here is the $2492 Classic Custom wagon.* **4.** *The '62 Americans were identified by a new "floating" grille up front and a dual-circuit "Double Safety" brake system underneath. On all '62 Ramblers, the 400 series replaced the Custom as the top trim level. The Custom became the new midline series, replacing Super. The 400 convertible was the year's most expensive American at $2344 to start.*

MAKE	TOTAL PRODUCTION	MKT POSITION
AMBASSADOR	36,171 ▲	
AMERICAN	125,678 ▼	4th ▼
CLASSIC	280,497 ▲	

SCORECARD 1962

4

AMERICAN MOTORS

1. *Another new grille design—this one with vertical bars—graced 1963 Americans. Model designations were revamped again; the lineup now ascended though 220, 330, and 440 models. The convertible body style was a 440-series exclusive.* **2.** *A two-door hardtop was a new addition to the American lineup. Like the convertible, it was available only in top-line 440-series trim. A fancier 440H model came standard with bucket seats and the "Power-Pack" 138-horsepower overhead-valve six. Hardtop shoppers found it a hard bargain to pass up; the H outsold the base model almost two-to-one. Regular hardtops, like the one pictured here, cost $145 less and came with a 125-hp version of the inline six.* **3.** *A chrome roof rack was standard on 330 and 440 wagons. Four-door wagons like the one pictured here were offered in all three trim levels, but two-door wagons came only in 220 and 330 trim.*

1. Rambler Classics and Ambassadors were new from the ground up for 1963, moving from a body-on-frame design to a unibody platform. Both models were offered in three trim levels: 550, 660, and 770 for Classics, and 800, 880, and 990 for Ambassadors. Classic 770s equipped with bucket seats could get the unusual "Twin-Stick" option, which got its name from the two shift levers that sprouted from the console. The one closest to the driver was a conventional shifter for the three-speed manual transmission, while the other was an in/out lever for the overdrive. **2.** Ambassador and Classic body styles included two-door sedans, four-door sedans, and four-door wagons, but no hardtops or convertibles. Though plusher and pricier, Ambassadors shared bodies and dimensions with Classics. The best-selling Ambassador, at 14,019 units, was the $2660 990 four-door sedan (shown). **3.** A full-length side-trim treatment graced the flanks of midlevel Classic 660 models. The 660 wagon came with a choice of six- or nine-passenger seating.

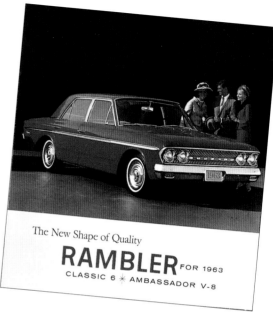

1. The six-cylinder Classic 660 four-door sedan was the top-selling 1963 Rambler by far, with 71,646 produced. This one wears Bahama Blue paint. The cutting-edge redesign made the new Classics and Ambassadors noticeably lower and wider. Curved side-window glass, a first in the Rambler's price class, aided appearance and opened up interior room. Innovative assembly techniques improved overall quality; one-piece "Uniside" door-frame structures were a Detroit first that saved weight, increased rigidity, and reduced squeaks and rattles. **2.** Classics came standard with a 127-horsepower, 195.6-cubic-inch inline six. For $105 more, they could get a 287-cid V-8 that made 198 hp. Ambassadors came standard with a 327-cid V-8 that made 250 hp; a 270-hp version was optional. Motor Trend magazine awarded its Car of the Year trophy to the entire 1963 Rambler lineup, the first time that AMC won that coveted honor. Led by its redesigned Classics and Ambassadors, AMC set sales and production records in 1963, but still fell to sixth in the industry sales race. **3.** Instrument panels featured an attractive "V" theme, with controls located on either side of the centrally located gauges.

SCORECARD 1963

MAKE	TOTAL PRODUCTION	MKT POSITION
AMBASSADOR	37,811 ▲	
AMERICAN	105,296 ▼	6th ▼
CLASSIC	321,019 ▲	

1. Classics and Ambassadors were updated for 1964 with a flat-faced grille, revised trim, and a two-door hardtop body style. Shown here is a Classic 770 Typhoon, a limited-edition intended to promote AMC's all-new 232-cubic-inch, 145-horsepower six-cylinder engine–the largest-displacement U.S.-built six then on the market. Only 2520 Typhoons were produced, all painted Solar Yellow with a Classic Black roof. **2.** Despite a substantial drop in sales from 1963, the six-cylinder 660 four-door sedan remained the single most popular Rambler Classic; 37,584 of the $2256 cars were built. **3.** All-new Rambler Americans, cleverly based on a shortened version of the 1963 Rambler Classic platform, were unveiled for '64. A full range of body styles was offered in three levels of trim: 220, 330, and 440. Prices started at $1964 and topped out with the $2346 ragtop (shown), which came only in 440-level trim. Styling was much improved over the boxy outgoing models.

1-2. The new Classic pushed the Ambassador upmarket, eliminating the 880 series. All Ambassadors were now 990s powered by the 327-cubic-inch V-8. Extra exterior brightwork was evidence of the Ambassador's top-line status; pictured here is the sportiest '64 Ambassador, the $2917 990H hardtop coupe. It came standard with bucket seats and AMC's most powerful engine of the year, a 270-horsepower version of the 327-cid V-8.

SCORECARD 1964		
MAKE	TOTAL PRODUCTION	MKT POSITION
AMBASSADOR	18,519 ▲	
AMERICAN	160,321 ▼	8th ▼
CLASSIC	206,299 ▼	

1. AMC was attempting to shed its stodgy image while still pitching practicality. Its 1965 lineup was dubbed "The Sensible Spectaculars." The cute Rambler American line saw minor trim changes and sporty add-ons such as bucket seats, floorshifters, and flashy wire wheel covers. Newly available for Americans was the 145-hp, 232-cid "Torque Command" six. **2.** The convertible body style was again exclusive to the top-line 440 series. It was the priciest American model at $2418 to start. **3.** This 440H hardtop coupe shows off the American's clean, uncluttered styling. The basic design was good enough to continue with only modest styling changes through 1969 and the end of the Rambler marque.

1. Ambassador's 1965 restyle brought squared-up lines with stacked headlamps—elements that also turned up an large Fords and Plymouths this year. Also new was a convertible body style. 2. The Ambassador line regained its exclusive longer wheelbase—116 inches, four inches longer than Classic. The 880/990 model range was also reinstated; pictured here is an 880 four-door sedan. Ambassador's standard engine was now the 232-cubic-inch six instead of a V-8, which was now optional.

1

2

3

SCORECARD 1965		
MAKE	TOTAL PRODUCTION	MKT POSITION
AMBASSADOR	64,145 ▲	
AMERICAN	109,134 ▼	8th ●
CLASSIC	199,063 ▼	
MARLIN	10,327 ●	

1-2. *The 1965 Classics were restyled with a convex "dumbbell" grille; recontoured hood; and a longer, squared-up rear deck. A convertible body style, exclusive to the top-line 770 series, was a new addition.* **3.** *Fastback styling was all the rage in the mid Sixties. AMC joined the trend by adding a swoopy fastback roof to its Classic body to create the Marlin. At $3100, it was the company's most expensive car. Sales were disappointing.*

'66 Rambler American

1. *The American lineup got new engines and a convertible body style for 1966. An attractive restyle included longer front fenders and a clean new grille. A 128-horsepower, 199-cubic-inch six was standard, a 232-cid six with 145 or 155 hp optional. Also optional was the line's first V-8, a 290 with a two-barrel carburetor and 200 hp, or a four-barrel and 225 hp. Asymmetrical rally stripes dressed up the ragtop in this ad, but were not a factory option.* 2. *The new Rogue was technically a separate model, but was really American's new upmarket entry. Note the unique roof/decklid two-tone paint scheme.* 3. *AMC badges replaced Rambler nameplates on the Marlin as AMC became a distinct make. Sales dropped even further from lackluster 1965—just 4547 were produced for '66.*

1

2

3

4

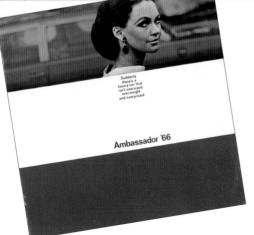

Suddenly
there's a
luxury car that
isn't oversized,
overweight
and overpriced.

Ambassador '66

SCORECARD 1966		
MAKE	TOTAL PRODUCTION	MKT POSITION
AMBASSADOR	71,692 ▲	
AMERICAN	93,652 ▼	9th ▼
CLASSIC	126,006 ▼	
MARLIN	4,547 ▼	

1. Like the Marlin, Ambassadors lost their Rambler name-plate and were marketed as AMCs for 1966. All got a mild retrimming. The $2968 990 convertible was the most expensive Ambassador. 2. The Ambassador DPL was a new special edition available only as a two-door hardtop. It came elegantly appointed with reclining buck-et seats, fold-down center armrests, pile carpeting, and many other standard features. 3. Much less ritzy was the 880 two-door sedan. At $2404, it was the cheapest Ambassador. It was also the least popular, with just 1493 built. 4. The 990 four-door sedan continued as the best seller in the Ambassador lineup. The price was down to $2574, output up to 25,986 units.

AMERICAN MOTORS

1. The 1967 Rogue retained the Rambler nameplate. A Rogue convertible was a '67-only addition. AMC was angling for the red-hot youth market with this gussied-up American, but even with two-tone paint and other frills, the Rogue looked staid compared with Ford's Mustang and Plymouth's Barracuda. **2.** The priciest '67 American was the $2533 440 station wagon. American engine options started with the 128-horsepower, 199-cubic-inch six and topped out with the 225-hp, 290-cid V-8. **3.** The '67 Marlin was switched to that year's new Ambassador platform and ended up much better proportioned on its longer wheelbase. Sales brochures boasted that the new Marlin had "The flair of a fastback, the luxury of Ambassador." Sadly, the improved styling didn't help sales, which plummeted again to a miserable 2545 units. The model was dropped for 1968.

1. The new-for-1967 Ambassadors were longer, lower, and wider, with curvier styling. The line-topping DPL trim level gained a convertible model. This one wears the optional silver-finished lower body. 2. With 12,552 orders, the DPL hardtop was the most popular two-door Ambassador. 3. A step down from the DPL was the Ambassador 990, a three-model line that included a Cross Country station wagon. Buyers had a choice of two- or three-seat configurations. 4. The Classic name was replaced with the Rebel monicker, but AMC's mainstream midsized cars retained their Rambler badges for '67. Shown here is the Rebel 770 Cross Country wagon.

1-2. *The sportiest 1967 Rebel was the top-line SST, which came in $2872 convertible (above) or $2604 hardtop form (below). Rebel shared its redesigned platform with the senior Ambassador. The handsome Richard Teague styling was highlighted by an inset rectangular grille, a "modified fastback" roofline, and a shapely rear deck with large, canted taillights. Newly optional for all Rebels was a 343-cubic-inch V-8 with 235 or 280 horsepower.*

REBEL FROM THE 1967 AMERICAN MOTORS

SCORECARD 1967

MAKE	TOTAL PRODUCTION	MKT POSITION
AMBASSADOR	62,839 ▾	
AMERICAN	69,914 ▾	9th •
MARLIN	2,545 ▾	
REBEL	100,627 ▾	

AMERICAN MOTORS

1-4. AMC rolled out a true sporty-car contender in the 1968 Javelin. Over 56,000 were built for '68, helping AMC out of a four-year sales slump. Styling was a fresh take on the long-hood/short-deck ponycar idiom, with sweeping C-pillars, flush door handles, and smoothly integrated bumpers. Base and SST trim levels were offered. AMC's 145-horsepower 232-cubic-inch six was standard; the 225-hp 290-cid V-8 was optional. Also optional was the "Go Package," which offered a 280-hp 343-cid V-8 with a four-barrel carb and dual exhausts, plus power front disc brakes, heavy-duty suspension, and wide tires.

1. AMC shortened the Javelin's 109-inch wheelbase by 12 inches to create the two-seat AMX at midyear. Engine choices ranged from a 225-horsepower 290-cubic-inch V-8 to a 315-hp 390. The latter did 0-60 mph in 6.6 seconds. The AMX's tight suspension, bucket seats, and standard 4-speed manual made it a capable semisports car. The base price was $3245, which was $1100 less than a Chevrolet Corvette, America's other two-seater. **2-3.** By 1968, Americans were the only AMC cars to retain the Rambler name. Rogue motored into the new model year with minimal changes. The top engine choice was again a 225-hp 290-cid V-8. Thin-stripe redline tires were a late-'60s ponycar/muscle car trend.

SCORECARD 1968

MAKE	TOTAL PRODUCTION	MKT POSITION
AMBASSADOR	54,651 ▼	
AMERICAN/ROGUE	80,982 ▲	
AMX	6,725 ●	9th ●
JAVELIN	56,462 ●	
REBEL	73,895 ▼	

1. Rebels lost their Rambler nameplates and became AMCs for 1968. The top series was again the SST, which consisted of just two body styles: the $2775 two-door hardtop (shown) and the $2999 convertible. **2.** Ambassador's big news was standard air-conditioning. At the time, A/C still cost extra on almost all American cars, even luxury makes like Lincoln and Cadillac. The 880 and 990 model designations were dropped, and SST was added above DPL as the top Ambassador series. Flush-mounted door handles were a subtle styling refinement on both Rebels and Ambassadors. Options on this Ambassador SST hardtop included wire wheel covers, bumper guards, and vinyl top. **3.** AMC's value-leader line for '68 was the Rebel 550 series, which included this hardtop coupe, two-door convertible, and four-door sedan, plus a four-door station wagon. The standard engine was a 145-horsepower, 232-cubic-inch inline six.

1-3. The American line and the Rambler nameplate took their final bows for 1969. Bidding both an outrageous farewell was the limited-edition '69 Hurst SC/Rambler. This was basically a Rogue hardtop carrying a big 315-horsepower, 390-cubic-inch V-8, a functional hood scoop, a four-speed manual transmission with Hurst shifter, heavy-duty suspension, and an outlandish red, white, and blue paint job. Priced at $2998, the "Scrambler," as it was inevitably nicknamed, was hardly sensible in the Rambler tradition, though it was a pretty spectacular junior muscle car. Published road tests confirmed AMC's claim of standing quarter-miles in the low 14s at around 100 mph. From rest, 60 mph came in a reported 6.3 seconds. Production was only 1512, though that was triple the planned run. A $61 AM radio was the sole option.

1. Most AMC race cars wore a bold red, white, and blue paint scheme, and a few streetgoing AMXs were decked out in the same motif. **2-3.** Eye grabbing shades of green, blue, or orange called "Big Bad Colors" were a midyear addition to the AMX and Javelin lineups. A mere $34 extra bought the wild paint, plus color-matched front and rear bumpers. This Big Bad Green AMX is an ultrarare California 500 Special. **4.** If Big Bad paint wasn't rousing enough, buyers could add sports options like a roof spoiler, side stripe, and faux exhaust rocker panel trim. This Javelin also sports fiberglass hood scoops, which were part of the optional "Go" Package. **5.** The Javelin nameplate migrated from the front fenders to the rear roof pillars for '69.

1. Ambassadors were restyled with a more-sculpted hood, plastic grille, and a return to horizontal headlights. Wheelbase grew by four inches to 122, topping that of the full-sized entries from Chevy and Ford. Base price of the SST two–door hardtop was $3522. 2. The Ambassador SST four–door sedan started at $17 less than the hardtop and was much more popular, with 18,719 sold. 3. Rebels, like this $2496 two-door hardtop, got a mild facelift for '69. 4. This 1969 issue of American Motors' official magazine depicts renowned race-team owner Roger Penske (left) and legendary driver Mark Donohue. AMC lured the winning Penske team to its SCCA Trans-Am Javelin program for the 1970 season.

SCORECARD 1969

MAKE	TOTAL PRODUCTION	MKT POSITION
AMBASSADOR	76,194 ▲	
AMERICAN/ROGUE	97,541 ▲	
AMX	8,293 ▲	9th ●
JAVELIN	40,675 ▼	
REBEL	60,106 ▼	

Chrysler Corporation ended the Sixties in much better shape than it began the decade. Detroit's perennial number three had flown high in the mid Fifties with bold "Forward Look" styling, race-winning Hemi V-8 performance, and innovations like "Torsion-Aire" ride. Then came the 1958 recession that changed buyer tastes overnight and all but obliterated the market for profitable medium-priced cars. By 1960, Chrysler was teetering on the brink, as it had several times since the Depression. Ford and General Motors took their lumps too, but Chrysler was locked into plans not easily or quickly changed.

The result through 1964 was a puzzling blend of the brilliant and bizarre. For example, all 1960 models save the luxury Imperials switched to "Unibody" construction, which promised fewer rattles than traditional body-on-frame, but was far more prone to early rusting. Valiant was the least popular of the Big Three's new 1960 compacts, yet Chrysler would have fared far worse without it. Even then, American Motors' compact Ramblers soon overtook the low-priced Plymouth to claim third in industry sales, after which Pontiac settled in. Tailfins, so *de rigueur* in the Fifties, were hastily shorn as passé. Managers also shed the "middle middle" DeSoto line after 1961, then let Chrysler and Dodge battle over its price turf. Chrysler's TorqueFlite was still one of America's best automatic transmissions, and the new-for-1960 "Slant Six" engines would prove long-lived winners. But the company blundered badly in deciding to abandon traditional "standard" Dodges and Plymouths for shrunken 1962 models with Valiant-like styling. The public was ready for midsized cars, but it didn't like these very much.

Racers liked them a lot, though, especially with a potent "ram-induction" 413 V-8, another 1960 innovation. Chrysler then revived Hemi power after a five year absence, and soon dominated NASCAR and drag racing. A Street Hemi option bowed for 1966 intermediates, just in the time for the "muscle car" wars.

By that point, Chrysler was into a successful new era under president Lynn Townsend, who took the reins from Tex Colbert in 1961, and design chief Elwood Engel, recruited from Ford to replace Virgil Exner in late 1961. With smooth, tasteful new Engel styling, full-range lineups, and a renewed emphasis on quality, Chrysler Corporation was again flying high by 1968. Helping the cause were popular additions like the Plymouth Barracuda, a "ponycar" to answer Ford's hugely successful Mustang; the burly midsize Dodge Charger, later immortalized by TV's *Dukes of Hazzard*; and other future icons like the Plymouth Road Runner and Dodge Coronet Super Bee. Chrysler also found time and money to continue its work with turbine engines, teaming with Ghia of Italy to create one of the most singular "production" cars ever.

In all, the Sixties was another roller-coaster ride for Chrysler Corporation. It would not be the last.

Inaugurated in 1955, Chrysler's high-performance "letter series" continued for 1960 with the 300-F convertible and hardtop coupe. A new 413 "wedgehead" V-8 with twin four-barrel carbs delivered 375 horses–400 with the "ram induction" manifolds shown here.

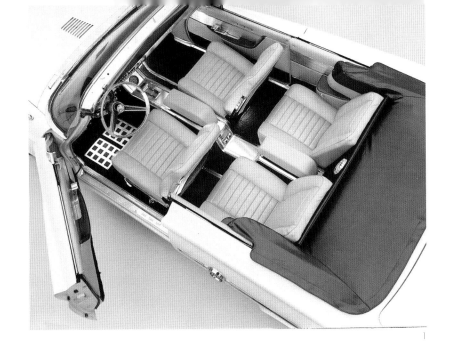

1. Four bucket seats and a full-length center console were standard for 300-Fs and a first for the letter-series Chrysler. Also new was an optional four-speed manual transmission by Pont-a-Mousson of France, though most 300-Fs left the factory with pushbutton TorqueFlite automatic. 2. All 1960 Chryslers had brand-new unibodies with soaring tailfins, but a distinctive "gun sight" grille was reserved for 300-Fs. Chrysler built just 1212 of its rapid limited edition this year, including a mere 248 convertibles, though that was an improvement on '59 production. 3. Windsor returned as Chrysler's entry-level line. The six-model 1960 series included this hardtop sedan, priced from $3343. Just 5897 were built. 4. The opulent 1960 New Yorker convertible saw only 556 copies; it sold for a princely $4975. 5. The most popular '60 Chrysler was the $3194 Windsor four-door sedan, which drew 25,152 sales. 6. The midrange Saratoga series included this hardtop coupe, one of four in Chrysler's 1960 lineup. Base price was $3989.

1

3

2

the new Dart, a full line of lower-priced "standard" Dodges effectively competing with Plymouth. This convertible and hardtop coupe were part of the top-trim Phoenix series. All models had rather busy styling that nevertheless fared well with the public. Dodge sold more than 323,000 Darts for the model year–tremendous "plus" business for dealers. Most models came with the sturdy new 225-cubic-inch corporate "Slant Six," but 318 and 383 V-8s were available, with Phoenix offering up to 330 horsepower.

4

1-2. After two years of sharp sales losses, DeSoto was reduced to just Fireflite and Adventurer series for 1960, each listing a four-door sedan, hardtop sedan, and hardtop coupe. All were basically retrimmed Chrysler Windsors with the same new 122-inch-wheelbase unibody–and lower prices than comparable '59 DeSotos. Adventurers like this hardtop coupe wore a bit more exterior chrome than Fireflites, but all were arguably handsome with their glassy rooflines, big trapezoidal grilles, and flying fins capped by "boomerang" taillamps. But none of this helped DeSoto sales, which skidded to some 26,000 for the model year. **3-4.** A bright spot in the 1960 corporate sales picture was

1-4. Dodge capped its 1960 line with new unibody Matador and Polara models. All used a 122-inch wheelbase, unchanged from '59, versus 118 inches for the new lower-priced Darts. "Seniors" also had unique styling and standard V-8. Representing the top-dog Polara group are this convertible, a pair of hardtop coupes, and a new pillarless "hardtop" wagon. Priced at $2900-$3600, these "senior" Dodges garnered just OK model-year sales of some 44,600 units. Polaras accounted for fewer than 17,000. **5-6.** A separate make since 1955, Chrysler's flagship Imperial was restyled for 1960, though the basic body and specific 129-inch-wheelbase chassis dated from 1957. The lone powertrain comprised a 350-horsepower 413 wedgehead V-8 and TorqueFlite automatic. Though arguably more contrived than 1957-59 styling, the '60 maintained Imperial signatures like a bold "eagle" nose emblem, "gun sight" taillamps, and a trunklid bulged to suggest a spare tire, a "classic" element of the sort favored by design chief Virgil Exner. This convertible and hardtop coupe were part of the midrange Crown series, which also listed a sedan and hardtop sedan, as did the base Custom and premium LeBaron lines. The $5774 convertible saw just 618 copies.

1

2

3

4

5

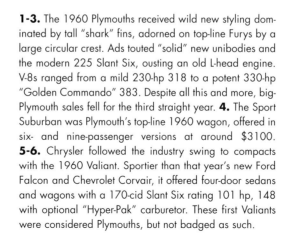

6

1-3. The 1960 Plymouths received wild new styling dominated by tall "shark" fins, adorned on top-line Furys by a
large circular crest. Ads touted "solid" new unibodies and
the modern 225 Slant Six, ousting an old L-head engine.
V-8s ranged from a mild 230-hp 318 to a potent 330-hp
"Golden Commando" 383. Despite all this and more, big-
Plymouth sales fell for the third straight year. **4.** The Sport
Suburban was Plymouth's top-line 1960 wagon, offered in
six- and nine-passenger versions at around $3100.
5-6. Chrysler followed the industry swing to compacts
with the 1960 Valiant. Sportier than that year's new Ford
Falcon and Chevrolet Corvair, it offered four-door sedans
and wagons with a 170-cid Slant Six rating 101 hp, 148
with optional "Hyper-Pak" carburetor. These first Valiants
were considered Plymouths, but not badged as such.

SCORECARD 1960

MAKE	TOTAL PRODUCTION	MKT POSITION
CHRYSLER	77,285 ▲	12th ●
DESOTO	26,081 ▼	13th ●
DODGE	367,804 ▲	6th ▲
IMPERIAL	17,719 ▲	15th ▲
PLYMOUTH	483,969 ▲	3rd ●

1

2

Chrysler '61

featuring the new
Newport
a full-size Chrysler in a
new, lower price range

3

1. An adroit facelift on the year-old unibody freshened Chrysler's looks for 1961. Immediately evident were an inverted trapezoidal grille and newly slanted quad headlamps above a straight-across bumper. Nonwagon models also received modified sheetmetal at the corners. New Yorkers like this $4175 hardtop coupe wore bright trim atop the front fenders and doors. 2. Chrysler wagons got the new '61 front end, but kept their previous tail styling. Wagons like this New Yorker Town & Country remained pillarless hardtop models. 3. Chrysler refused to offer a compact like rival medium-priced brands in '61. Instead, it issued the Newport line of lower-priced full-sized cars. The four-door sedan listed at an eye-opening $2964, and was predictably the most popular '61 Chrysler with more than 34,000 sales. 4-5. Styling was the main difference between 1961's high-performance 300-G and the previous year's F. Production was again limited, but a bit higher at 1617 hardtops and convertibles.

4

5

1-2. DeSoto died in November 1960 after a token '61-model run of 3034 units. Only a two- and four-door hardtop were offered with a fairly clumsy Chrysler-like facelift. DeSoto had by now outlived its usefulness, its place in the corporate scheme lately usurped by less costly Chryslers and higher-priced Dodges. **3.** Dodge Darts like this Phoenix convertible got a heavy restyle for '61, surprising for a year-old design. The new look was somewhat controversial, which may explain why Dodge sales fell 35 percent for the model year, the Dart line sustaining most of the loss. **4.** Dodge got into compacts for 1961 with Lancer. Basically a retrimmed Valiant, it offered seven models divided between 170 and 770 series. Both included a four-door wagon like this, plus a four-door sedan and new two-door sedan. The 770 added a hardtop coupe, also new for '61 and shared with Valiant. Despite similar pricing, Lancer was far less popular than Valiant.

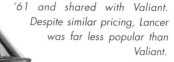

1-2. Highlighting Dodge Dart's extensive 1961 restyle were a wide concave grille, peaked front fenders, and curious "reverse" tailfins that tapered toward the rear. If not the last word in taste, these cars were judged more attractive than their '61 Plymouth relatives. **3-4.** This year's premium Dodges were pared to a single line of Polaras styled almost exactly like Darts. It seemed an odd thing to do, but Chrysler was short on cash, and marketers likely felt the visual similarity would help Dart sales–which it didn't. Polara did keep a longer wheelbase, however, plus an airy hardtop wagon versus Dart's pillared type. The Polara wagon was Dodge's priciest '61, listing at $3294 with seating for six or $3409 in nine-passenger form. But none of the six models sold well and the Polara line dropped to 14,032 model-year deliveries, some 2700 fewer than lackluster 1960.

1-2. Imperial managed only some 12,300 sales for 1961, down by over 5700 despite fresh styling for the second time in as many years. Eliminating pillared sedans didn't help. Neither did a new look featuring "classic" freestanding headlamps in separate chrome bullets, taller "shark" tailfins, and some unusual sheetmetal sculpting. This $5403 Crown coupe was one of five "standard" models, all but one of them hardtops. Custom Imperial limousines remained available to special order. **3.** Any '61 Imperial was a rare sight. Even the top-selling Crown hardtop sedan saw only 4769 copies. **4.** Priced at $5774, the Crown convertible was the rarest of '61 Imperials, with just 429 built. **5.** The top-line LeBaron was down to just a hardtop sedan for '61. Again wearing a limousinelike "formal" rear roof, it started at $6426. Imperial's gun sight taillamps now dangled from the fins, but this was the only time they would. A standard deck-lid spare tire motif returned to complement the new retro headlamp design, but this twain would never meet again.

1, 3, 6. Full-sized Plymouths received a startling 1961 makeover marked by finless rear fenders and a frankly odd front end. Designers were striving for a different look, but this was too much, and Plymouth sales plunged 22 percent from 1960, itself a disappointment. Pictured here are the $2967 Fury convertible and two midrange offerings, the Custom Suburban four-door wagon and Belvedere four-door sedan. *2.* Valiant returned for its second season wearing Plymouth badges. It also got a few cosmetic changes and two new body styles: this jaunty hardtop coupe in the uplevel V200 line, and a two-door sedan in base V100 trim. The hardtop started at $2137 and drew nearly 18,600 sales. *4.* The V200 sedan was again the top-selling Valiant with over 59,000 units for '61. *5.* Wagons, by contrast, remained Plymouth's least popular compacts with just 6717 V100s and 10,794 V200s like the one shown here.

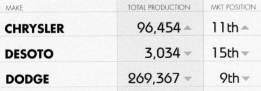

SCORECARD 1961

MAKE	TOTAL PRODUCTION	MKT POSITION
CHRYSLER	96,454 ▲	11th ▲
DESOTO	3,034 ▼	15th ▼
DODGE	269,367 ▼	9th ▼
IMPERIAL	12,258 ▼	14th ▲
PLYMOUTH	356,257 ▼	4th ▼

1. Chrysler shaved off tailfins for 1962 and replaced midrange Windsors with a "nonletter" 300 line of convertibles, four-door sedans, hardtop coupes, and hardtop sedans. The 300 Sports looked much like this year's high-power 300-H, but a standard 383 V-8 and fewer luxury trappings allowed much friendlier prices of $3300-$3900 versus $5000-plus. Buyers endorsed these other moves, and Chrysler-brand sales jumped by over 33 percent for the model year to almost 129,000. 2. Town & Countrys went finless by adopting rear sheetmetal from '61 Plymouth wagons. It was another hasty but clever bit of mix-and-match body engineering necessitated by last-minute cancellation of an all-new '62 Chrysler. Wagons sales remained sluggish, though. This New Yorker Town & Country is one of 8905 built. 3. The four-door sedan remained the most popular New Yorker, attracting just under 10,000 sales for '62. New Yorker's convertible and hardtop coupe were dropped, leaving a four-door hardtop as the only other offering. 4. A 1962 "family portrait" from Chrysler PR poses a new Imperial LeBaron with a trio of Chryslers (from left): New Yorker sedan, 300 hardtop sedan, and Newport Town & Country wagon. All these cars were sometimes called the "plucked chickens" after a term coined by design chief Virgil Exner, who was gone by '62.

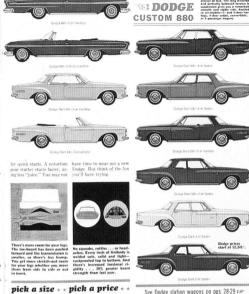

This automobile is probably unlike any you have ever driven, seen or read about.

It's two feet shorter than America's longest car and two feet longer than America's shortest car. It's right in the middle.

For a fact it's one of the quickest cars going. You can feel the difference instantly. Feel it in the powerful Slant Six or V-8 engines.

Yet for all its zip and snap, it doesn't backslide from economy one inch.

While acceleration is up as much as 10%, gas mileage is improved as much as 7%.

Dodge Dart is more fun to drive for 1962. It's easier to

handle and easier to park. And, with Dodge's new low-friction steering gear, you get the easiest turn this side of power steering. Even a 96-lb. woman can drive without extra stress or strain.

Inside the new size Dart—room. Plenty of headroom and legroom for a family of six. And plenty of comfort any way you mix them. (In the Dart 440, the center armrest folds down and gives you the security of a bucket seat. Need more room? Fold it up again.

YOU'LL KNOW IT'S A DODGE WHEN YOU TRY TO WEAR IT OUT

Bodies are fully unitized and rustproofed, inside and out. (For extra protection, galvanized steel is used in critical areas.) You'll go 32,000 miles on one grease job, 4,000 miles before you change the oil. Dodge brakes adjust themselves automatically every time you back up and step on them.

The Alternator charges at all speeds, even at idle. Makes the battery last longer, keeps it up to snuff

sion system (rated by the experts as the finest in any American car) has been further improved to protect the car from body-wearing bumps and jolts—gives you even smoother handling on rough roads and curves.

The Torsion-Aire suspen-

for quick starts. A reduction gear starter starts faster, using less "juice." You may not

have time to wear out a new Dodge. But think of the fun you'll have trying.

There's more room for your legs. The toe-board has been pushed forward and the transmission is smaller, so there's less hump. You get more stretch-out room for your legs whether you move them from side to side or out in front.

No squeaks, rattles . . . or headaches. Every inch of Unibody is welded safe, solid and tight—rustproofed top to bottom. And there's increased torsional rigidity . . . 30% greater beam strength than last year.

DODGE
Polara 500

This special edition, full-size Dodge is not for everybody. It's got a walloping 361 cubic in. V-8 engine, four barrel carburetor, special camshaft, and dual exhausts. It comes as a convertible (shown left) or as a 2- or 2-door hardtop. The interior is unadulterated luxury. Saddle-grain vinyl throughout. Adjustable bucket seats in the convertible and 2-door hardtop have pleated inserts. Thick rugs. The works.

pick a size ★ ★ pick a price ★ ★
PICK A DODGE!

*Manufacturer's suggested retail price for Dodge Dart 2-door sedan, exclusive of destination charges. White sidewalls, wheel covers optional extra.

See Dodge station wagons on pgs. 28-29

1. *Believing General Motors was about to shrink its "standard" cars, Chrysler issued much smaller Dodges and Plymouths for 1962. But GM didn't downsize, and buyers didn't much like the new Chrysler models, so Dodge hastily restored full-sized cars at midseason. Called Custom 880 for no particular reason, these were basically '62 Chrysler Newports with '61 Dodge Polara front ends. This ad sums up the model-year story with the tagline "Pick a Size. Pick a Price. Pick a Dodge!" Despite the planning fumble, Dodge actually scored higher model-year sales versus dismal '61.* **2-4.** *Dodge used the Dart name for its downsized '62 standards. Pride of the line was the new Polara 500, shown here as a hardtop coupe and convertible. There was also a hardtop sedan. All featured sporty bucket seat interiors and specific exterior trim. Other Darts were arrayed in base, 330, and 440 series. All rode a trim 116-inch wheelbase. A standard 225 Slant Six made a modest 145 hp, but gave decent go in these relatively light cars. Available V-8s ranging up to big-block 413s could make for a real fire-breather, as drag racers were quick to note. Polara 500s listed for $3000-$3200, and were the rarest '62 Darts with 12,268 built, including just 2089 ragtops.*

1962 DODGE DART 440 SPORTS-SWEEP

1-2. Though mainstream buyers largely shunned the '62 Dodge Darts, law enforcement liked these trimmer, lighter cars for their tidier handling and higher performance potential versus full-sized rivals. Speed demons liked them for the same reasons. As if to court them all, Dodge offered a 413 "Max Wedge" V-8 with dual quad carbs, "Ramcharger" manifolds, and 410 hp. It was strictly a "special use" option, expensive and seldom ordered, making this deceptively plain-looking two-door sedan a very rare survivor. **3.** Continuing Chrysler Corporation's longtime practice of offering sales-boosting "spring specials," Dodge added a "Sports-Sweep" package as a midyear option for '62 Dart 440s. Slim upper-body color spears and rear-fender hashmarks furnished the look of top-line Polara 500s at much lower cost. **4-5.** Taking note of Chevrolet's hot-selling Corvair Monza compacts, Dodge gave the Lancer 770 hardtop a natty bucket-seat interior, extra brightwork, and the larger 145-hp 225 Slant Six. The resulting Lancer GT listed from $2257, but was not a big draw, managing only 13,683 sales. All '62 Lancers got a new grille and other trim changes, but were basically carryovers.

1. Last-minute thoughts also ended plans for an all-new '62 Imperial, but designers managed a tasteful restyle despite little time. A divided grille à la 1955 models is evident on this Crown hardtop coupe, which sold for $5400. 2. Rear-end appearance changed even more dramatically, as the befinned fenders of 1961 were planed to horizontal and topped by "gun sight" taillamps that also recalled 1955. This year's Crown convertible wore the new look especially well, but drew only 554 sales at $5770 each. 3. Visual dignity was also served by eliminating the "toilet seat" trunklid, as passé as tailfins by 1962. The change was especially apt for the grand $6422 LeBaron hardtop sedan. 4. Plymouth, like Dodge, began 1962 relying heavily on smaller standard cars, but wasn't allowed to resurrect full-sized models, due to its showroom pairing with Chrysler. However, the Plymouth line did get mid-season spice with a revived Sport Fury, a hardtop coupe and convertible with snazzy bucket-seat interiors and a standard 305-hp 361-cid V-8 instead of a Slant Six.

1

2

SCORECARD 1962

MAKE	TOTAL PRODUCTION	MKT POSITION
CHRYSLER	128,921 ▲	11th ●
DODGE	240,484 ▼	9th ●
IMPERIAL	14,337 ▲	14th ●
PLYMOUTH	339,527 ▼	8th ▼

meet a new Plymouth Sport Fury!

3

1-2. Plymouth's mainstream '62 standards ranged from a basic $2206 six-cylinder Savoy two-door to a jaunty $2924 Fury convertible with standard 318 V8. Most critics thought styling a big improvement over '61, but buyers balked at the new models' greatly reduced size, to the detriment of total Plymouth sales. 3. This brochure announced the Sport Fury's midyear return. The bucket-seat twosome attracted a meager 5555 sales, including just 1516 convertibles. 4. With sporty compacts all the rage, the Valiant Signet 200 was a timely 1962 addition. Like Dodge's Lancer GT, it was basically the prior year's hardtop spruced up with vinyl bucket-seats inside and special cosmetic touches outside. Priced from $2230, the Signet outsold its Dodge cousin, racking up 25,586 model-year orders. 5. Plymouth's '62 full-line catalog began with a plea that seemed a bit desperate, even at the time. Then again, Plymouth was way behind traditional rivals Ford and Chevrolet in the sales race.

4

Look at Plymouth now!

5

1,4. Chrysler touted the "crisp, new, custom look" for a 1963 restyle inspired partly by the aborted all-new '62 design. All models now strode a 122-inch wheelbase. **2-3.** A Chrysler was chosen to pace the 1963 Indy 500, and the division celebrated with a specially equipped 300 "Pace Setter" convertible and hardtop coupe. Respective production was 1861 and a paltry 306. **5.** Another "spring special," the New Yorker Salon hardtop sedan delivered power everything; cruise control, vinyl roof, and more for $5860. Only 563 were sold.

1-2. Chrysler had been working on gas turbine engines in modified Dodges and Plymouths since the mid 1950s. In 1963, the company began loaning out 50 specially built hardtop coupes for consumer evaluation. Equipped with the latest fourth-generation engine, the Turbine Car was styled by recently hired design chief Elwood Engel. Bodies were crafted by Ghia in Italy. The evaluation program ended in early 1966 with mixed reviews, but Chrysler would keep working with turbines through 1980. Because of U.S. tax laws, all but three Turbine Cars were destroyed, but the survivors are still around.

3-4. Darts were simply "Dodges" for 1963–and arguably more attractive thanks to fast work by new design chief Engel. A three-inch-longer wheelbase enhanced the crisp new lines on non-wagon body styles, like this pair of Polara 500 hardtop coupes. The new look helped total Dodge sales, which nearly doubled for the model year.

1. Dodge reinstated a standard Polara line with a full range of body styles for 1963. The most glamorous model was this spiffy convertible, listing at $2963 with standard 318-cubic-inch V-8. The 440 and 330 series each moved down a notch on the price scale. 2. The midsize Dodge dashboard remained a slim, space-saving affair with useful needle gauges for amps and oil pressure, not warning lights as on most competitors. 3-6. Detroit was officially back to selling high-performance iron by 1963 after several years of promoting safe driving while providing under-the-table support to various

favored race teams. Dodge contested this new "horsepower race" with midsized cars packing some heavy new artillery. The familiar 383 V-8 was now available in four versions with horsepower ratings of 305, 320, 325, and 330–depending on compression ratio and carburetor count. Dodge also unleashed a quartet of "Ramcharger" 426 wedgehead engines set up to deliver 370, 375, 415, and 425 hp. Many Ramchargers went racing, sometimes on the street. There, a low-line 330 two-door with oversize tires and jacked-up suspension, as shown here, was a sight to be feared if you were in something else. As if all this weren't enough, Chrysler announced a new hemi-head V-8 late in the '63 model year, a 426-cid bruiser sold only for racing. Horsepower was a nominal 425, but was probably more like 475 or 500 actual by the optimistic SAE gross measurement then in use. All this firepower served notice that Dodge and sister Plymouth were out to beat General Motors and Ford on any stock car track or dragstrip–as they mostly did in '63 and especially 1964.

1. The full-size Dodge Custom 880 got a fresh face for its first full season. Also new for '63 were a lower-priced standard-trim 880 sedan and wagon. Though big-Dodge sales still weren't huge at about 28,000 for the model year, dealers made good money on each one. **2.** Dart became a compact for 1963, replacing Lancer with crisp Elwood Engel styling on a more generous 111-inch wheelbase (106 for wagons). Convertibles were added in GT and midrange 270 trim. Two- and four-door sedans remained the mainstay sellers; the base 170 two-door now started at just under $2000. With fresh looks and reliable Slant Six engines–standard 170 cubic inch or optional 225–Dodge

compact sales nearly doubled to a smashing 154,000 for the model year. **3-4.** Imperials marked time for 1963 with minor changes in appearance and features. Sales eased by a few hundred units, but that was good going for a basic design that was now eight years old. Model choices were unchanged, as was the lone 340-hp 413 V-8. As before, all models, bar the Crown convertible, were Southampton hardtops. This four-door Crown repeated as the line's top-selling model, drawing 6960 orders at $5656 each.

1. At over 488,000, Plymouth's 1963-model sales were the highest since '57. Reskinned standards with crisp, "correct" lines played a big part in that. The top-line $3082 Sport Fury convertible looked especially good, but persuaded only 3836 buyers. **2.** Fury, midrange Belvedere, and low-line Savoy again rounded out the standard Plymouth lineup. **3.** A squared-off roofline à la Ford Thunderbird marked '63 Plymouth sedans and hardtops. This Sport Fury was one of 11,483 built. **4.** Four-door sedans accounted for over half of 1963 standard Plymouth sales. This Belvedere tallied 54,929. **5.** New race-tuned 426 "Super Stock" V-8s powered Plymouths to the top ranks in 1963 NHRA drag racing. Tom Grove won trophies with his Melrose Missle III.

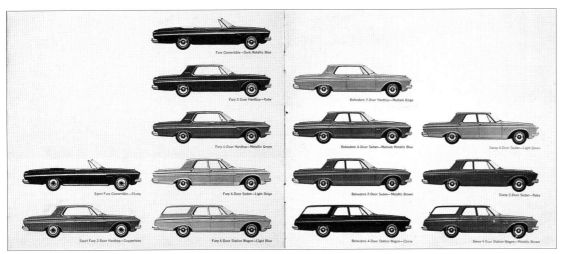

Fury Convertible—Dark Metallic Blue

Fury 2-Door Hardtop—Ruby

Belvedere 2-Door Hardtop—Medium Beige

Fury 4-Door Hardtop—Metallic Green

Belvedere 4-Door Sedan—Medium Metallic Blue

Savoy 4-Door Sedan—Light Green

Sport Fury Convertible—Ebony

Fury 4-Door Sedan—Light Beige

Belvedere 2-Door Sedan—Metallic Brown

Savoy 2-Door Sedan—Ruby

Sport Fury 2-Door Hardtop—Coppertone

Fury 4-Door Station Wagon—Light Blue

Belvedere 4-Door Station Wagon—Ebony

Savoy 4-Door Station Wagon—Metallic Brown

SCORECARD 1963		
MAKE	TOTAL PRODUCTION	MKT POSITION
CHRYSLER	128,937 ▲	11th ●
DODGE	446,129 ▲	8th ▲
IMPERIAL	14,121 ▼	14th ●
PLYMOUTH	488,448 ▲	4th ▲

1. A letter-series ragtop was absent for 1963, but rejoined the hardtop coupe as a 300-K. 2. All 1964 Chryslers wore a mild facelift, as on this New Yorker sedan. 3. Ads pitched the surprising affordabilty of full-size Chrysler luxury in 1964. 4. Hardtop wagons were in their last year. This New Yorker saw fewer than 2800 sales. 5. A midyear "Silver Special" trim option for 300 and 300-K hardtop coupes drew respective sales of 2152 and 255.

1. Another fresh face and a restyled rear end marked Dodge's full-sized '64s. Models were again grouped in a single 880 line comprising a base sedan and pillared wagon and a Custom sedan, hardtop wagon, hardtop coupe and sedan, and convertible. This price-leader 880 sedan was a lot of metal for the money at $2826 to start. **3.** Dodge kept on pushing the 880 in 1964, just to make sure everyone knew it had full-sized cars to sell. Although volume jumped almost 20 percent for the model year, to nearly 32,000, Chrysler sold over twice as many of its similar Newports. **2.** The compact Dodge Dart got a convex grille as part of an expected second-season facelift, but the big news was an optional 273 V-8 with 180 hp. Light, efficient, and revvy, it was perfect for sporty Dart GTs like this hardtop. Dodge compact sales made a smart gain to over 193,000 for 1964.

1

1-3. New lower-body sheetmetal gave 1964 midsized Dodges more of a "big car" air. Polara and Polara 500 hardtop coupes also received a distinctive V-shaped roofline with "slantback" contouring that added valuable top-end speed for stock car racing. A redesigned dashboard graced interiors on all models. This 500 hardtop doesn't look like much a high-performance car, but under its hood lurks a 365-hp 426 wedge V-8. It also has the optional console-mount four-speed floorshift with Hurst linkage. **4.** Dodge built a handful of Hemi-engined '64s for use at "sanctioned" dragstrips. This 330 two-door is one of them. Note the unique functional hood scoop, plus the fat tires and high-rise suspension. These Dodges were fierce competitors–and usually in the winner's circle. Jim Thornton's "Candymatic" Ramcharger, for example, won the National Hot Rod Association's 1964 U.S. Nationals.

2

3

4

1. Imperial finally cast off all vestiges of the Fifties with a handsome 1964 redesign. It looked much like contemporary Lincoln Continentals–no surprise, as Elwood Engel had helped shape those cars before joining Chrysler. The Crown convertible now listed at $6003. Only 922 were built. **2-3.** The Crown hardtop coupe was the most affordable '64 Imperial at $5739, but drew just 5233 sales. Its four-door sister sold nearly three times better. A 340-hp 413 remained the sole Imperial engine. **4.** Plymouth restyled again for '64 and watched total sales soar past the half-million mark. The Sport Fury hardtop more than doubled its sales, reaching 23,695. **5.** Slicker hardtop styling helped Richard Petty and his Hemi-powered Belvedere to win the 1964 NASCAR championship in a breeze. Plymouth ads, meantime, promised plenty of high-performance thrills for Sport Fury owners.

1,3,4. Arriving in spring 1964 as an early '65 model, the fastback Barracuda was a clever variation on Plymouth's year-old second-generation Valiant. That it went on sale within days of Ford's Falcon-based Mustang was sheer coincidence, though Chrysler knew of Ford's "ponycar" as its own sporty compact neared completion. Aimed at the same fast-growing youth market as Mustang, the Barracuda sported specific front-end styling and front bucket seats. Beneath a huge "glassback" window was a fold-down rear seat that allowed carrying a surfboard inside with the stubby trunklid closed, or so Plymouth claimed. A Slant Six was standard, but the optional 273 V-8 accounted for over 90 percent of "1964½" sales, which totaled 23,443.
2. The Belvedere four-door sedan remained the top-selling standard Plymouth for 1964, attracting over 57,000 customers.

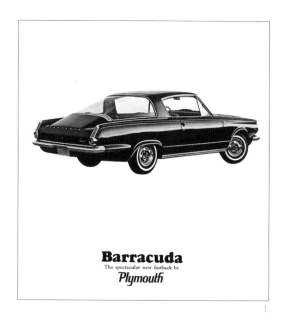

Barracuda
The spectacular new fastback by
Plymouth

1

4

3

SCORECARD 1964

MAKE	TOTAL PRODUCTION	MKT POSITION
CHRYSLER	153,319 ▲	11th ●
DODGE	501,781 ▲	6th ▲
IMPERIAL	23,295 ▲	14th ●
PLYMOUTH	551,633 ▲	4th ●

1. In a banner year for all Detroit, the Chrysler brand enjoyed record sales for 1965, besting 206,000 units. Larger dimensions and suave new styling were key factors in that showing. This year's New Yorker hardtop coupe priced from $4161 and drew 9357 orders. **2.** Listing at $4618, the 300-L convertible was the rarest '65 Chrysler with just 440 built. The letter series was by now almost identical with regular 300s, so the Ls were the last of the original breed. **3.** The Newport convertible started at $3442 for '65 to remain Chrysler's best-selling ragtop, though it wasn't exactly common with just 3142 built. **4.** The 300 hardtop coupe drew 11,621 sales at $3551 each. The $3911 ragtop version notched only 1418.

1

3

4

5

2

6

1-2. Dodge Darts got a more-extensive facelift for 1965, and more performance from a newly optional 235-hp V-8. The sporty GT convertible and hardtop coupe again topped the line. **3.** Dodge revived the Coronet name for a restyled fleet of midsize '65s pitched directly at Ford's Fairlane and Chevrolet's Chevelle. This Coronet 500 hardtop coupe delivered a bucket-seat interior and a 180-hp V-8 for $2674, before options. **4.** The Coronet 500 also came as a convertible priced from $2894. Midsize-Dodge power options this year ranged from the Dart's new 235-hp 273 V-8 up through 361, 383, and 413 engines. King of the hill was a 365-hp 426 wedgehead. **5.** Arrayed below Coronet 500s were base, Deluxe, and 440 models spanning all the usual body styles save a hardtop sedan. A bench-seat convertible was exclusive to the 440 line, listing from $2622 with standard Slant Six. **6.** Coronet scored over 209,000 sales, the best ever for a midsize Dodge. This is the popular 440 wagon.

1

2

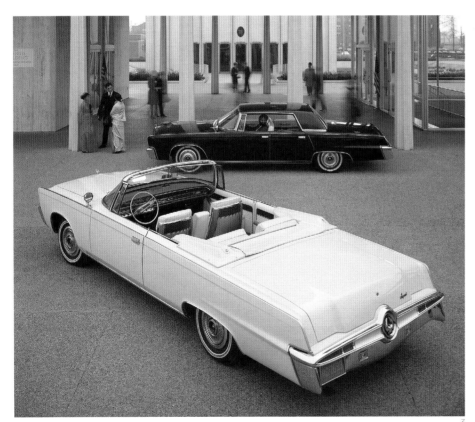

1. Dodge greatly expanded its full-size line for 1965 with all-new Polaras and Custom 880s. Each series offered a convertible, four-door sedan, wagons, and two- and four-door hardtops covering a wide $2806-$3527 price spread. A special Polara 318 sedan included a 230-hp V-8 for just $2730. Others had a standard 270-hp 383. Customs like this ragtop delivered nicer trim and more standard features for $200-$270 more than Polaras. All used a new unibody platform shared with Chryslers and Plymouth Furys, but used an intermediate 121-inch wheelbase. Sales were decent at 57,201 combined. About four out five were Customs. **2.** A new big-Dodge confection was Monaco, a personal-luxury hardtop coupe to challenge the likes of Pontiac Grand Prix. Starting at $3335, it came with a 315-hp 383 V-8, plus a dashing vinyl interior with center shift console, brushed-metal trim, and rattan wicker inserts on the door panels and the backs of front bucket seats. Sales totaled 13,096. **3-4.** Predictably, few changes were made to the year-old Imperials, though glass-covered headlamps were a new touch shared with uplevel '65 Chryslers. Model-year sales dropped nearly 21 percent, reflecting stiff competition from an all-new Cadillac. Here, the Crown hardtop sedan, convertible, and hardtop coupe.

3

4

1. Looking tastefully elegant fronting the Chicago skyline, this 1965 Imperial hardtop sedan originally listed for $5581. This model remained the most popular of Chrysler's flagships with 14,181 built . **2.** Imperial's middecade dashboard was a far cry from the overstyled "spaceship" panels of the Fifties and early Sixties. A wide "strip" speedometer was typical of the age, but note the needle gauges and switch console arrayed below. The dashtop pod mounts an automatic headlamp dimmer, an option first seen in the 1950s. **3.** Plymouth finally returned to true full-sized cars with all-new 1965 Furys. These were carefully calculated to match the largest Fords and Chevrolets, from an identical 119-inch wheelbase to handsomely square "formal" styling and spacious interiors. Unibody construction, however, was still unique to Plymouth among the "Low-Priced Three." A bucket-seat Sport Fury hardtop coupe and convertible led the line at $2960/$3209. Respective production was 38,348 and 6272. **4.** A step below on Plymouth's big-car ladder was the Fury III, offering a full range of body styles including a convertible and this $2863 hardtop sedan. It was Plymouth's most popular big-car line, drawing as many sales as the lower-priced Fury II and Fury I sedans and wagons combined. Reviving true full-sized cars considerably improved Plymouth sales, which soared to over 728,000 for the model year.

1. A 1965 Fury was the first Plymouth ever chosen as pace car for the Indianapolis 500. **2.** The vintage-'62 standard Plymouth was restyled and recast for '65 as the "new" mid-size Belvedere line. Satellite denoted the top-shelf bucket-seat convertible and hardtop. Mainstream models were called Belvedere I and II. Sales were good at over 164,000, but well below the '64 level when Plymouth had no true full-sized cars. **3.** Plymouth's popular compact Valiants got another mild facelift for '65. Convertibles reprised a bucket-seat Signet and this $2437 bench-seat "200." **4.** Barracuda added an optional Formula S package for '65 featuring a firmer suspension and a 235-hp V-8. The fastback drew some 65,000 sales. **5.** The popular Valiant 200 four-door sedan started at $2195 this year.

SCORECARD 1965		
MAKE	TOTAL PRODUCTION	MKT POSITION
CHRYSLER	206,089 ▲	10th ▲
DODGE	489,065 ▼	7th ▼
IMPERIAL	18,409 ▼	14th ●
PLYMOUTH	728,228 ▲	4th ●

1. Chrysler sales improved by over 58,000 units for 1966 to reach nearly 265,000. The 300 convertible, though, remained a low-demand item, as only 1418 were built this model year. 2. All '66 Chryslers received a lower-body facelift, but only New Yorkers like this sedan offered a big new 440-cubic-inch V-8 with 350 standard horses or 365 optional. 3. Chrysler dropped New Yorker wagons for '66 after years of sluggish demand, but reprised six- and nine-passenger Newport Town & Countrys. They drew fewer than 18,000 sales this season, but that wasn't bad for big cushy cars costing $4100-$4200. 4. Chrysler put new rooflines on its '66 hardtops to set them apart from sister Dodges and Plymouths. Two-doors like this 300 got a "slantback" style. Sales of Chrysler's sportiest models jumped no less than 79 percent to nearly 50,000. Newport and New Yorker rose too, besting 167,000 and 47,000, respectively, despite a modest sales retreat for Detroit as a whole.

1

2

1-3. Buyers had rediscovered 1940s-type fastback styling by 1966, and Dodge responded to their interest with the Coronet-based Charger hardtop coupe. Hidden headlamps and full-width taillamps were also slated for other '66 Coronets, but were scratched at the last minute. As a result, the Charger arrived early in the calendar year as a separate one-model series. A mild 230-hp 318 V-8 was standard, but a 325-hp four-barrel "Magnum" 383 was optional. So was a new street-legal version of the racing 426 Hemi, rated at 425 hp. Charger drew 37,344 debut-year sales, with the 383 option accounting for most. The unique interior offered front bucket seats, full-length center console, and individual rear seats that folded down for near station wagon load space.

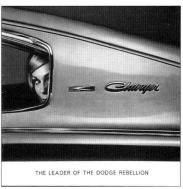

THE LEADER OF THE DODGE REBELLION

3

1

2

3

CORONET

4

5

JOIN THE DODGE REBELLION

'66 DODGE CORONET

6

1. Dodge Coronets were redesigned for 1966, switching to freshly styled unibodies on an unchanged wheelbase. Trim levels again ascended through base, Deluxe, 440, and bucket-seat 500. This 440 convertible listed at $2672 with Slant Six, $2766 with the base 180-hp 273 V-8. **2.** Coronet styling was both crisper and more flowing for '66. The squarish lower body lines with "hopped-up" rear fenders were inspired by the new Charger fastback. Delta-shaped taillamps provided a visual link with full-sized Dodges. This 500 hardtop coupe stickered at $2611/$2705 with six/V-8. **3.** Despite tough midsize competition, Dodge sold over a quarter-million '66 Coronets, nearly a 20-percent year-to-year gain. One of the most popular individual models was the Coronet 400 sedan, priced from $2432/$2526. There was also a first-time 500 sedan at $2586/$2680. **4.** Coronet 500s and other midsized Dodges were also available with the new Street Hemi, as well as 318, 361, and 383 V-8s. This 500 convertible priced from $$2827/$2921. **5.** The compact Dodge Darts got another style freshening for '66, but sales did not improve this time; indeed, they fell by some 33,500 to 176,027. Here, the GT convertible. **6.** Dodge marketing aimed at the go-go youth market in 1966 with "The Dodge Rebellion" theme.

1. Dodge's full-sized Custom 880s were renamed Monaco for '66. Polaras remained a notch lower in price and opulence. All sported fresh lower-body styling announced by a "dumbbell" grille with fine vertical bars. 2. The makeover also included broad "delta wing" taillights, as on this Monaco 500, the renamed '66 version of Dodge's big personal-luxury hardtop. The model drew about 2250 fewer sales this season, ending at 10,840. 3. The main 1966 changes for Imperial involved an eggcrate grille and a standard 440 wedgehead V-8 with 350 hp. The bigger big block made only 10 horses more than the previous 413, but allowed Imperial to pass Cadillac in the "displacement race," though Lincoln's 462 was still the largest in the luxury class. Imperial sales declined again, easing to 13,742. This Crown hardtop coupe accounted for 2373. 4. Plymouth's total sales skidded below 684,000. Full-sized cars fell 14 percent to 282,500. Fury IIIs, like this hardtop sedan, remained the most popular. All received a modest facelift. 5. Answering the Chevrolet Caprice and Ford LTD was the new-for-1966 Plymouth VIP, a pair of top-line hardtops with standard vinyl roof, rear fender skirts, luxury interiors, and 318 V-8. This two-door listed at $3069, the four-door at $3133.

1,3. Midsized Plymouths were redesigned for '66, with sporty Satellites again topping the line. NASCAR banned the Hemi in 1965 because it wasn't "production," hence the '66 Street Hemi option, which included heavy-duty suspension. The reinstated racing Hemi took Richard Petty to victory in the Daytona 500. **2.** Valiants wore squarish new lower-body lines for '66. Here, the sporty $2261 Signet 200 hardtop. **4.** Barracudas got a blockier nose and a new "fighting fish" logo. The Formula S performance package remained a "must" option for enthusiasts.

Power play.

The new 1966
Plymouth Satellite.

Let yourself go... *Plymouth*

SCORECARD 1966

MAKE	TOTAL PRODUCTION	MKT POSITION
CHRYSLER	264,848 ▲	10th ●
DODGE	632,658 ▲	5th ▲
IMPERIAL	13,742 ▼	13th ▲
PLYMOUTH	687,514 ▼	4th ●

1,5. Concave bodysides marked a more extensive restyle for 1967 Chryslers. So did a new hardtop-coupe roofline with wide, vision-reducing rear pillars. "Affordable luxury" got a renewed push from new deluxe-trim Newport Customs, a sedan, and two hardtops pitched about $200 upstream of equivalent Newports. The Customs were supposed to boost volume, and found a respectable 50,000 buyers, but most of that was cannibalized from the 300 line, which plunged over 50 percent for the model year. Total sales retreated by 46,000 to just under 219,000. **2-3.** The hardtop coupe was 1967's most popular 300 at 11,566 units. Vertical taillamps, a peaked grille, and "spinner" hubcaps were unique to this year's models. A newly standard 440 V-8, available for Customs, delivered 350 standard hp, 375 optional. **4.** Newport Town & Countrys gained an inch in wheelbase, but were still two inches short of other models in that dimension. An optional trailering package and rear air conditioning were worthwhile for wagons. Available front disc brakes were a wise investment on any model.

1,2,5. Dodge formally entered the fast-growing "muscle car" market with a fast-moving 1967 Coronet R/T ("Road/Track") hardtop coupe and convertible. Standard were a 375-hp 440 big-block V-8, stiff suspension, bigger brakes and tires, and a deluxe bucket-seat interior. They were just what the market seemed to want, yet total Dodge sales plunged 26 percent for the model year to just under 466,000. **3.** All '67 Coronets received a minor facelift of their new-for-'66 styling. The sporty 500 returned with a four-door sedan, this hardtop coupe, and a convertible with standard Slant Six and available V-8s up to a 325-hp 383. Unhappily for Dodge, this series suffered a 29-percent drop in model-year sales to 39,260 units. **4.** Charger sales fared even worse for '67, diving 58 percent to 15,788. A mere six dollar hike in base price was among a handful of changes for the sophomore edition.

1. *Dart was redesigned for 1967, gaining more of a "big car" look without altering wheelbases. The new unibodies had room for big-block V-8s, and a few drag racers stuffed them in, but the factory's top performance option remained the 235-hp 273 small-block. This GT convertible listed for $2860 with the base 180-hp V-8, $2732 with the reliable Slant Six. For all the new finery, however, Dart sales were down about 20,000 for the model year to some 154,500.* **2.** *Mainstream Darts again comprised 170 two- and four-door sedans and 270 four-door sedans and hardtop coupes. The 270 sedan remained a family favorite, with sticker prices starting at $2362.* **3.** *Dodge gave its full-sized '67s a heavy facelift featuring a busy front end, more pronounced lower-body sculpturing, and even larger delta-wing taillamps. A 270-hp 383 V-8 was standard across the board. Wagons again came in both Polara and uplevel Monaco trim.* **4.** *Big Dodges gained an inch of wheelbase for '67, going to 122, and seven inches in overall length. They picked up no sales, though: Volume declined to just under 119,000, a loss of over 52,000. The luxury-leading Monaco 500 hardtop drew 5237 orders this model year.*

1. Imperial finally shed body-on-frame construction with a clean-sheet 1967 redesign based loosely on the Chrysler unibody. Wheelbase was longer, though, at 127 inches. Fresh styling was also unique to the flagship line. The main-stay Crown series reinstated a pillared sedan, but the pillar-less four-door remained the sales leader at 9415 units. This Crown convertible is one of just 577 sold at $6244 each.
2. The Imperial LeBaron continued as a high-luxury four-door hardtop with "formal" roofline. It listed from $6661 for 1967 and drew 2194 sales. 3-5. A clean-sheet redesign made the '67 Plymouth Barracuda a true "ponycar" to rival Ford's Mustang. Hardtop coupe and convertible body styles moved from the Valiant line to join a restyled fastback that many thought looked rather "Italian." Though Mustang was still far ahead in sales, Barracuda model-year volume shot up by over 64 percent to some 62,500 units.

coupes offered two roofline styles: this thin-pillar type and a "Fast Top" with wide triangular pillars. **2-3.** The big '67 news among midsized Plymouths was a distinct muscle car, the Belvedere GTX. Starting as a Satellite hardtop coupe or convertible, it came with a torquey 350-hp "Super Commando" 440 V-8 and offered the 425-hp Street Hemi at extra cost. Also featured were beefed-up suspension, fat tires on styled-steel wheels, and special trim that included a pair of nonfunctioning hood scoops. The big air intake on this car is a modification for drag racing, but the dorsal racing stripes were a factory option. At $3200-$3400, the GTX was quite a deal. **4.** As ever, a low-line Belvedere I two-door was a lighter and stealthier home for one of Plymouth's high-power engines.

1. Plymouth was "out to win you over" for 1967, but ended up winning some 49,400 fewer sales than in '66, the total amounting to some 638,000. The loss was hard to fathom, given an impressive lineup led by handsomely restyled full-sized cars like these Sport Furys. Hardtop

SCORECARD 1967		
MAKE	TOTAL PRODUCTION	MKT POSITION
CHRYSLER	218,742 ▼	10th ●
DODGE	465,732 ▼	7th ▼
IMPERIAL	17,620 ▲	13th ●
PLYMOUTH	638,075 ▼	4th ●

For the man who wouldn't settle for a second-best anything.

Compared with other wagons, Chrysler's Town & Country isn't a wagon at all. It's sort of the penthouse of luxury cars. With feature after standard feature you'd expect to be optional.

363 cubic inch V-8 with automatic transmission.

Power brakes and power steering. All-vinyl interiors. Complete carpeting.

Getting the picture? Town & Country is a world apart from the plain-vanilla wagons. And its options let you pile luxury on luxury. Add a 7-position steering wheel. Power windows. Power door locks. Six-way power seat.

And three options nobody else has. A 3-in-1 divided seat with passenger-side headrest and recliner. Dual air conditioners.

And a tail gate window that washes itself. So if you're looking for just an ordinary wagon, look somewhere else.

But if you really want your wagon to be as much limousine as loadspace, you've only got one choice. Chrysler's Town & Country. Make your move.

MOVE UP TO CHRYSLER

CHRYSLER

1. Chrysler focused on styling for 1968–and meeting new government safety and emissions standards mandated for all cars. Despite little news, sales improved by a healthy 24 percent to almost 265,000. Town & Country wagons were again restricted to the entry-level Newport line. 2. Newly hidden headlamps enhanced visual width on '68 Chrysler 300s. The convertible rose less than $100 in base price to $4337, but remained a rare bird with just 2161 sales for the model year. 3. Two-door '68 Newports added an interesting midseason option: wagonlike "Sportsgrain" simulated-wood side paneling. The price was nice at $126, but only 965 hardtop coupes and a mere 175 convertibles were so equipped. 4. The fed's new rules included front and rear side-marker lights. They were quite discreet on this 300 hardtop and other Chryslers.

1-5. Big Dodges looked cleaner for 1968. The Polara and Monaco lines again listed hardtops, four-door sedans, and wagons seating six or nine, but ragtops were still reserved for Polara. A sporty Polara 500 hardtop coupe and convertible, reinstated for '67 after several years off, returned with the lush Monaco 500, but combined sales didn't break 10,000. **6.** Dodge labeled its hottest '68s the "Scat Pack" cars and gave them identifying "bumblebee" tail stripes. Among them was a very quick new Dart GTS hardtop coupe and convertible with a standard 275-hp 340 V-8; a 300-hp 383 was available. **7-8.** A lot more people caught "Dodge Fever" for '68. Dart sales rose 11 percent, and total Dodge sales zoomed almost 35 percent. **9.** This Hemi-powered Dart is one of about 80 specially produced for NHRA Super Stock drag racing.

1-2. The midsize Dodge Charger morphed from fastback to "tunnelback" with a 1968 redesign that scored more than 96,000 sales–six times the previous model-year volume. From hidden headlamps to curvy bodysides to a neatly clipped tail, this Charger looked ready to race in NASCAR–and it did with great success. "Bumblebee" tail stripes marked the hot R/T ("Road/Track") version (right) that delivered a 375-hp Magnum 440, firm suspension, fat tires, and special trim from $3506. The unstriped $3040 base model (left) came standard with a 230-hp 318 V-8. **3.** Another new "Scat Pack" '68 was the Coronet Super Bee, a no-frills muscle car priced from just $3027, a sizable $300-$600 less than Coronet R/Ts. Sold only as a fixed-pillar coupe, Super Bee came with a stout 335-hp Magnum 383 V-8, but the 426 Street Hemi was optional, if rarely ordered. It was another showroom attraction that pumped up the sales action for Dodge dealers. **4-5.** Like Charger, Coronet was clean-sheet new for '68, wearing smoother, more flowing lines of its own. The desirable R/T convertible returned at $3613, the hardtop coupe at $3379. Combined sales were modest at 10,849.

1. After moving up to near 18,000, Imperial sales moved down again for 1968, settling at around 15,400. This year's LeBaron hardtop sedan drew just 1852 orders. **2.** The '68 Crown would be Imperial's last convertible. Priced from $6497, it found a mere 474 customers. **3.** The Crown hardtop sedan remained the most popular Imperial, the '68 finding 8492 buyers. **4.** Plymouth's second-generation Barracuda got minor trim changes for second-season '68. The Formula S option graduated to a standard 275-hp 340 V-8. A 300-hp 383 was also newly available. This convertible is one of only 2840 built for the model year. **5-6.** An optional "mod top" vinyl roof cover and matching interior trim gave the Barracuda hardtop a little "flower power" for '68. **7.** Valiant also settled for cosmetic tweaks after its '67 makeover. Models were down to two- and four-door sedans in base 100 and shinier Signet trim.

1

2

3

1,2. Midsized 1968 Plymouths adopted a smoother look on a new platform shared with Dodge Coronets. The posh, potent GTX hardtop coupe and convertible returned as a separate series atop a reordered lineup. Sales were modest at 18,940, but total Plymouth volume jumped by some 152,000 units to break 790,000. *3.* Plymouth popularized the "budget muscle car" with its new '68 Road Runner, a Belvedere coupe or hardtop coupe packing a 335-hp 383 V-8, tight suspension, taxicab-plain interior, and a "beep beep" horn sounding like the famous cartoon character. At around $3000 to start, the Road Runner was a bona fide performance bargain that attracted 44,599 happy, leadfoot customers. *4.* The big Plymouth Furys were mildly freshened for '68. This Sport Fury "Fast Top" pillarless two-door started at $3225.

4

SCORECARD 1968

MAKE	TOTAL PRODUCTION	MKT POSITION
CHRYSLER	264,853 ▲	10th ●
DODGE	627,533 ▲	6th ▲
IMPERIAL	15,367 ▼	13th ●
PLYMOUTH	790,239 ▲	4th ●

1. Chrysler said it had "your next car" for 1969, but its redesigned "fuselage styled" models drew some 4000 fewer sales than the '68s. The makeover did not change wheelbases, but did add width and length–not to mention weight. Still, a nice blend of curves and creases helped offset the greater visual mass of higher bodysides. The "Sportsgrain" trim on this Newport convertible was a dealer-installed item for '69, not a factory option, but it makes this example all the more special, as only 2169 ragtop Newports were built that year. Base price for the model was up to $3823. **2.** The soft-top 300, Chrysler's other convertible, was a perennial slow seller too, and would disappear with the open-air Newport after just 1933 orders for '69. Hidden headlamps remained exclusive to all 300s, but they now nestled in a massive loop-type combination bumper/grille.

Dodge Scat Pack ... the cars with the Bumblebee stripes

1-2. Dodge's sexy Charger entered 1969 with subtle visual changes, most noticeably a split grille and rectangular tail-lamps. Base Chargers (above) could be equipped with a 330-hp four-barrel 383 V-8. The sporty R/Ts (below) came standard with a 440, and could be ordered with the mighty 426 Hemi. Hard to believe, but a lowly Slant Six was still available on base models if you insisted. Most buyers didn't. Orders fell below 90,000–unsurprising, as most all-new cars post a second-season sales loss. **3.** This year's Coronet R/T hardtop started at $3442, but cost far more when ordered with a rip-snorting Hemi, which got a twin-scoop "Ramcharger fresh air induction system" hood. This is one of but 97 hardtops so equipped. **4.** Seeking maximum mph in 1969 NASCAR racing, Dodge added a $3860 Charger 500 with a flush rear window that reduced high-speed air drag versus the stock "tunnelback." An even more aerodynamic Charger Daytona added a towering rear wing and a "droop snoot" nose to win a fair share of races, but not the NASCAR crown.

1969 Dodge Polara.
Totally new, it is. Expensive, it isn't.

1. Redesigned big cars led by sporty Polara 500s were the newest way to catch "Dodge Fever" in 1969. Still, total Dodge sales retreated to just under 612,000. 2,4. Darts got a modest restyle for '69, but demand for the hot GTS hardtop and convertible cooled to 6702 units. 3. For weekend drag racers--and stoplight drag racing--Dodge offered a "Six Pack" option for the Super Bee at midseason. The no-nonsense package included a flat-black lift-off fiberglass hood secured by four hood pins, unadorned steel wheels, and a triple-two-barrel carburetor version of the 440 V-8 that put out 390 horsepower. 5. All Coronets got a mild freshening for '69. This hardtop was one of 7208 R/Ts built, each looking like the proverbial iron fist in the velvet glove.

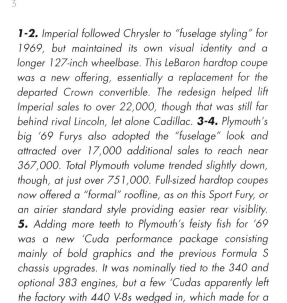

1-2. Imperial followed Chrysler to "fuselage styling" for 1969, but maintained its own visual identity and a longer 127-inch wheelbase. This LeBaron hardtop coupe was a new offering, essentially a replacement for the departed Crown convertible. The redesign helped lift Imperial sales to over 22,000, though that was still far behind rival Lincoln, let alone Cadillac. **3-4.** Plymouth's big '69 Furys also adopted the "fuselage" look and attracted over 17,000 additional sales to reach near 367,000. Total Plymouth volume trended slightly down, though, at just over 751,000. Full-sized hardtop coupes now offered a "formal" roofline, as on this Sport Fury, or an airier standard style providing easier rear visiblity. **5.** Adding more teeth to Plymouth's feisty fish for '69 was a new 'Cuda performance package consisting mainly of bold graphics and the previous Formula S chassis upgrades. It was nominally tied to the 340 and optional 383 engines, but a few 'Cudas apparently left the factory with 440 V-8s wedged in, which made for a fast but frightening handful even in a straight line.

1-3. Plymouth's "budget" muscle car became a bit less so for 1969, adding nicer appointments and a $3313 convertible version. The likely reason for this was to make up for declining sales of the Road Runner's premium-priced GTX stablemates. The strategy worked: While GTX sales declined this year by some 3300 to 15,602, the beep-beep car almost doubled volume to sell more than 84,000, which more or less offset the lower profit on each Road Runner sold. As it was still possible to get a plain pillared coupe for around $3000, Road Runner hadn't entirely abandoned its original low-price/high-performance mission.

SCORECARD 1969		
MAKE	TOTAL PRODUCTION	MKT POSITION
CHRYSLER	260,773 ▾	10th ●
DODGE	611,645 ▾	7th ▾
IMPERIAL	22,103 ▴	13th ●
PLYMOUTH	751,134 ▾	4th ●

FORD MOTOR COMPANY

After birthing the biggest automotive flop of the 1950s, Ford Motor Company promptly sired the two biggest hits of the Sixties. Dearborn also captured the public imagination with its "Total Performance" assault on most every form of motorsport—including the storied 24 Hours of LeMans, which it won four years running (1966-69). The program also produced some of the hottest, most memorable road cars of the era.

There was nothing especially memorable about the Falcon, but it was far and away the most popular of the Big Three's new 1960 compacts, and remained a strong seller through decade's end. Though some models were quite sporty, Falcon always had a refreshing simplicity that led many to think of it as a latterday Model A. And thanks to the ill-starred Edsel, Ford had enough factory space from day one to build all the Falcons the market wanted—which was quite a lot.

Early Falcons were the sort of no-nonsense cars favored by Ford chief Robert S. McNamara, who briefly served as company president before joining the Kennedy Adminstration. By the time he left in late 1960, family scion Henry Ford II had made himself chairman and installed a hot-shot salesman named Lee Iacocca at Ford Division. With help from new corporate design chief Eugene Bordinat, Iacocca fast shifted the Blue Oval from dull to dynamic, symbolized best by the youthful mid-1964 Mustang "ponycar," the low-cost sporty compact that became an instant American icon.

Ford had other "better ideas" that were less spectacular in commercial terms, but important nonetheless. For example, a near-moribund Lincoln got a new lease on life in the luxury field with the elegant 1961 Continental. And medium-priced Mercurys moved far beyond their traditional "deluxe Ford" status to encompass everything from big-power Cyclones to Lincoln-like full-sized cars to sporty European-inspired Cougars, all with a special character found only at "The Sign of the Cat." Let's also not forget that Ford pioneered the mid-size car with its 1962 Fairlane and built a slew of street-legal race cars just to satisfy racing rules, performance legends like the Boss 302 and Boss 429 Mustang, Torino Talladega, and Mercury Cyclone Spoiler.

In all, Ford was at the top of its game in the 1960s. And if that didn't trump mighty General Motors in sales, Dearborn was, for a few brief shining years, the center of the gearhead's universe.

1. Edsel bowed for 1958 as its own make positioned between Ford and Mercury. Bad timing, middling quality, and awkward styling spelled the marque's doom. Following a dismal 1958 and '59 model year, Ford pulled the plug in November '59 after a token 1960 model-year run of just 2846 cars. Only 76 were convertibles like this one. 2. Station wagons were called Villagers and held up to nine passengers. 3. The 1960 Edsels were basically retrimmed versions of that year's all-new full-sized Fords, as this Ranger two-door hardtop illustrates. 4. This small brochure listed 70 Edsel selling points. Part of the small print disclaimer on the back page read, "Edsel Division of Ford Motor Company reserves the right to discontinue models at any time." 5. The Ranger four-door sedan was the best-selling Edsel at 1288 units.

70 big reasons to go Edsel in '60

1. Ford scored big with the Falcon, one of 1960's new Big Three compacts. Simple, affordable, and easy on gas, Falcon rang up nearly 436,000 sales to trump Chevy's rear-engine Corvair and Plymouth's odd-looking Valiant. Pictured is the four-door sedan, which started at just $1974. **2.** Ford's largest cars were fully redesigned for 1960, becoming longer, lower, and wider on a one-inch-longer wheelbase (now at 119). Styling was cleaner than ever. The $2860 Sunliner convertible drew 44,762 sales this season. The chrome windsplit seen here was a rarely ordered dealer accessory. **3.** Galaxie returned from 1959 as the top-line nonwagon series. Among its five models was this Town Victoria four-door hardtop, priced from $2675. **4.** The flagship of Ford's station wagon lineup was the $2967 Country Squire. The "wood" bodyside trim was actually Di-Noc woodgrain transfers bordered by lighter-grained fiberglass sections. **5.** The four-seat "Squarebird" was three years old in 1960, yet sales improved to nearly 91,000, a mark that wouldn't be bettered for several years. Rear-fender hashmarks and a revised grille were part of a mild facelift.

1-2. Dearborn's flagships differed only in detail for 1960, but sales sank to just under 25,000 for Lincoln and Continental combined, the lowest total since 1948. Continentals, now called Mark V, remained the crème de la crème. This year's Mark Vs again shared a burly 430 V-8 with Lincoln standard and Premiere models, but recession-prompted detuning cut horsepower by 35 to 315. The Continental hardtop sedan retained its reverse-slant roofline and power-down rear window. *3.* Lincoln's behemoths rode an imposing 131-inch wheelbase, 1.5 inches longer than Cadillac's and an inch longer than Imperials. This is the $5696 Premiere two-door hardtop. *4-5.* At a lofty $7056, the Continental convertible was the most expensive standard model. Nineteen sixty was the finale for the big unibody Lincolns introduced for '58.

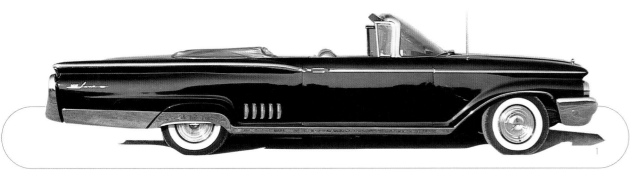

1. The Park Lane convertible was the priciest and rarest of the 1960 Mercurys. Just 1525 of the $4018 ragtops were built.
2. Big-M wagons thinned from four to two for '60. The Commuter was available in six- or nine-passenger forms.
3. Colony Park wagons returned with woody-look side trim and luxury appointments. Starting price was $3837–big money in 1960. **4.** The Monterey convertible sold for almost $1000 less than its Park Lane sibling. The 312- and 430-cid V-8s, standard depending on the series, were slightly detuned from '59. **5.** Mercury's only full-size two-door sedan was in the Monterey lineup. Though its starting price was attractive at $2631–the lowest in the line–the model drew a modest 21,557 sales. Rear fender skirts were rare on period big Detroit sedans, but were factory available on these Mercs.

SCORECARD 1960		
MAKE	TOTAL PRODUCTION	MKT POSITION
EDSEL	2,846 ▼	17th ▼
FORD	1,439,370 ▼	2nd •
LINCOLN	24,820 ▼	14th ▲
MERCURY	271,331 ▲	8th ▲

FORD

1. A deft lower-body reskin gave full-sized 1961 Fords a simple, pleasing new look. Large, round taillamps returned after a year's absence. A clean new concave grille used a horizontal bar ahead of a "polka-dot" background whose texture was simply stamped-in rather than composed of multiple buttons. Accessory rear fender skirts adorn this Sunliner convertible. **2.** Ford's big-car instrument panel remained simple and slim for '61, contributing to bountiful passenger room. All-vinyl trim was standard on Sunliners, as shown here. **3.** A T-Bird-style squared-off roofline again capped line-topping Galaxie models like this $2664 Town Victoria four-door hardtop. Expanding big-Ford engine options was a new 390-cid V-8 offering 300 horsepower standard, with 330, 375, and a mighty 401 hp available. **4.** The heaviest and costliest non-Thunderbird was the 4015 lb, $3013 nine-seat Country Squire. Sales reached 22,237.

1-2. The '61 Thunderbird was new from road to roof and striking from any angle. Wheelbase and overall size didn't change much, but everything else did. Ford's new 300-hp 390 V-8 was the sole engine, and was well up to the car's two-ton heft. A standard Swing-Away steering wheel eased entry and exit. Hardtops priced from $4172, a sizable $417 above the 1960 version. Though some said it looked rocketlike, the '61 T-Bird was less fussy and more coherent than the jazzy 1958-60 models. **3.** Adding dash to the '61 Falcon line was the midyear Futura two-door with vinyl bucket-type front seats and a Thunderbird-style center console, plus unique wheel covers and rear fender trim. It was priced from $2162, $248 above the regular two-door. Ford introduced the model to counter the Corvair Monza, Chevrolet's popular sporty variant of its compact car. The seeds of the forthcoming ponycar revolution were being planted.

1-2. A complete break with the past, the all-new 1961 Lincoln Continental was much smaller and lighter than the outsized 1958-60s—and arguably much more handsome. Indeed, its styling—directed by Elwood Engel—won several coveted awards for design excellence. The model line was simplified to consist of a sole trim level in two body styles. The four-door sedan featured a thin B-pillar and curved, frameless door glass. It accounted for the bulk of the '61 Continental's 25,164 sales. **3-4.** The other body style was a four-door convertible, the first in the U.S. since the 1951 Frazer Manhattan. It cost $6713 and weighed 5215 pounds. Its rear-hinged decklid swallowed the power top, making for a clean top-down appearance. The new Lincolns rode a 123-inch wheelbase, eight inches shorter than their 1958-60 predecessors. Both body styles had rear-hinged "suicide" doors, a 300-hp, 430-cid V-8, and much improved workmanship. The success of these cars rescued Lincoln from near extinction and established a cohesive design theme that would carry the make through the rest of the decade.

1. Mercury's compact Comet gained a sporty S-22 model for 1961. Its special features included bucket seats and a console, two-tone steering wheel, and unique wheel covers on narrow-band whitewalls. **2.** Responding to a shrunken medium-price market, full-sized Mercurys were reorganized into low-priced Meteor 600 and 800 models, a premium Monterey series that included this $3128 convertible, and a parallel station wagon line. These smaller, lighter, more rational Mercurys seemed just right for the times, but model-year sales actually fell, skidding below 121,000, the worst showing since 1948. **3.** Mercury made prototypes of a 1961 Montclair four-door hardtop sedan (shown), but the upscale Montclair series was canceled and the model was never produced. The four-door hardtop body style did see the light of day, but as a less ritzy Monterey model.

1

2

SCORECARD **1961**		
MAKE	TOTAL PRODUCTION	MKT POSITION
FORD	1,338,790 ▾	1st ▴
LINCOLN	25,164 ▴	13th ▴
MERCURY	317,351 ▴	7th ▴

3

FORD

1. Another lower body reskin gave a fuller, "more important" look to Ford's full-sized cars for 1962. Galaxie now denoted the most affordable sedans; a new upscale Galaxie 500 line also listed hardtops and this Sunliner convertible. **2.** The $2667 Galaxie 500 four-door sedan was Ford's most popular car, with 174,195 produced. **3.** The second most popular full-size Ford was the $2674 Galaxie 500 hardtop coupe, which rang up 87,562 sales. **4.** The Falcon Futura became even more "mini T-Bird" at mid 1962, when its roofline went from rounded to angular. A new "electric shaver" grille freshened Falcon's front-end styling. **5.** Falcon's '62 Deluxe models had more bright exterior trim than base versions, including a broad swath of ribbed aluminum on the lower rear fenders. Despite somewhat lower model-year volume, Falcon remained America's top-selling compact car.

1-2. Ford unearthed more marketing gold by stretching its compact into a new Fairlane sized between Falcon and full-sized Fords. It bowed with two- and four-door sedans in plain and fancy 500 trim, plus a bucket-seat 500 two-door sport coupe. Falcon's larger six was standard, but two new Challenger V-8s were available: a 145-hp 221 and a lively 164-hp 260. Fairlane got off to a strong start with more than 297,000 sales. **3.** Thunderbirds got mildly revised trim and a gutsy new engine option for 1962. For an additional $242, buyers could choose a 340-hp version of the 390 V-8 with triple Holley two-barrel carburetors. The hardtop coupe started at $4321. **4.** Answering pleas for another two-seat T-Bird was the new Sports Roadster, basically the regular ragtop with a removable fiberglass tonneau hiding the rear seat. The forward end of the integral headrests mated with the tops of the front seats. Genuine wire wheels were included in the $5439 price, but not the rear fender skirts seen here. The hefty price tag likely limited sales, which reached a paltry 1427.

1. Lincoln promised that its "New Frontier"-era Continental would not be changed willy-nilly. Sure enough, the follow-up '62s were but subtly refined. The most obvious differences were repositioned headlamps and a new pattern for the grille and back panel. Buyers seemed to approve as model-year sales bested 31,000. **2.** Lincoln called its 1962 Continental "a remarkable investment," and indeed the convertible would prove to be exactly that over time. Compared to 1961, the price edged up only $47, to $6720, while the weight, already a hefty 5215 pounds in 1961, increased to an even portlier 5370. This made the Lincoln 740 pounds heavier than the Cadillac Series Sixty-Two two-door ragtop, even though the Caddy measured about ten inches longer overall. **3.** Despite a relatively large interior, slim center door posts, and no fixed top, Continental convertible sedans were surprisingly solid and quiet.

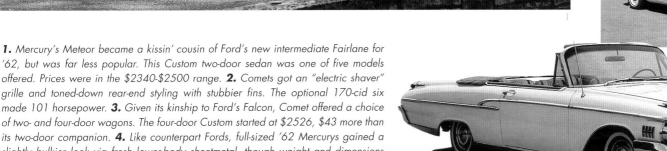

1. Mercury's Meteor became a kissin' cousin of Ford's new intermediate Fairlane for '62, but was far less popular. This Custom two-door sedan was one of five models offered. Prices were in the $2340-$2500 range. 2. Comets got an "electric shaver" grille and toned-down rear-end styling with stubbier fins. The optional 170-cid six made 101 horsepower. 3. Given its kinship to Ford's Falcon, Comet offered a choice of two- and four-door wagons. The four-door Custom started at $2526, $43 more than its two-door companion. 4. Like counterpart Fords, full-sized '62 Mercurys gained a slightly bulkier look via fresh lower-body sheetmetal, though weight and dimensions didn't change significantly. 5. All nonwagon big Mercurys were Montereys for '62, but there were now standard and uplevel Custom series, each with a selection of sedans and hardtops. This Custom hardtop coupe was priced from $2972.

SCORECARD 1962

MAKE	TOTAL PRODUCTION	MKT POSITION
FORD	1,476,031 ▲	2nd ▼
LINCOLN	31,061 ▲	13th •
MERCURY	341,366 ▲	7th •

FORD

1

2

3

4

1. Ragtop Galaxie Sunliners returned for '63 in bucket-seat XL and bench-seat regular models. A small front-fender badge signals the new 427-cubic-inch big-block V-8 option available for most big-Ford models. **2.** Ford still liked to call itself "America's Wagonmaster," and its '63 caravan was the broadest ever. The woody-look Country Squire remained the biggest and brightest of the bunch, again offered with two or three rows of seats. At midyear, Galaxie 500/XL front bucket seats, console, and other interior trim became a first time option for Country Squires, which priced from $3018. **3.** Station wagon shoppers on a tighter budget could choose the Country Sedan wagon, which started at $2829. The six-passenger version was Ford's most popular wagon, with 64,954 sold. **4.** Semifastback Galaxie 500 hardtop coupes bowed at midyear to replace the Thunderbird-like roof. The new roofline's slicker aerodynamics were a big plus in long- distance stock car races, combining with competition-tuned big-block V-8s to make Ford the season champ in NASCAR. (Tiny Lund drove one to victory in the 1963 Daytona 500.) This "slantback" XL packs the hot tri-carb 406 mill, good for up to 405 hp.

1. Thunderbird was spruced up for '63 with a new grille pattern and a prominent bodyside creaseline that flattened the top of the front wheel arches. **2.** The Thunderbird Sports Roadster returned for 1963, again at a whopping $700 premium over the standard convertible. Sales dropped more than two-thirds, to just 455. **3.** Fairlanes were facelifted with a new grille that mimicked their full-sized Ford counterparts. This is the $2242 Fairlane 500 two-door sedan. **4.** A new two-door hardtop body style was exclusive to the Fairlane 500 line-up. **5.** Fairlane wagons were another new addition for '63; the $2781 faux "woody" Squire was the priciest. **6.** Available V-8 power, two-door hardtops, and convertibles were new for Falcon. This convertible is the top-line Sprint version, which included the 164-hp 260 V-8, stiffer suspension, and a dashtop-mounted tachometer. **7.** A four-door sedan was new to the Falcon Futura line. With 31,376 built, it was the most popular member of its newly enlarged series. **8.** Just 4269 Falcon Deluxe two-door wagons were made for '63.

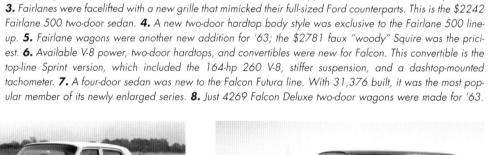

1

1. Another new grille and an increase of 20 horsepower–to 320–were the significant changes made to the 1963 Lincolns. Sales of convertibles declined minutely, but demand for the sedan was nudged forward, just past the 28,000 mark. Base prices for both Continental models were increased by $196 for the year. 2. Like sister Fords, full-sized '63 Mercurys were handsomely restyled below the beltline and offered more model variations. Wagon offerings were scaled back to include only woody-look Colony Parks in $3295 six- or $3365 nine-passenger forms. 3. Recalling the 1957-1958 Turnpike Cruiser was a bevy of new 1963 "Breezeway" hardtops and sedans. All featured a rear window that dropped at the touch of a button to assist interior ventilation. Nobody, not even Ford, offered anything like them. Pictured here is the $3650 Monterey Custom S-55 hardtop coupe. Full-size Mercury engine choices ranged from a 250-hp 390 V-8 to a 410-hp 427.

2

3

SCORECARD 1963

MAKE	TOTAL PRODUCTION	MKT POSITION
FORD	1,525,404 ▲	2nd ●
LINCOLN	31,233 ▲	13th ●
MERCURY	301,581 ▼	9th ▼

1. *The midsize Mercury Meteor was facelifted for 1963, and sprouted wagon models and a pair of hardtop coupes. Wagons offered six- or eight-passenger versions, though third-row accommodations were a bit cramped. The woody-look Country Cruiser started at $2886.* **2-3.** *Meteor hardtop coupes came in two forms: the $2448 Custom (top right) and the sportier bucket-seat S-33 version, which started at $2628. The former outsold the latter 7565 to 4865.* **4.** *Like Falcon, Mercury's compact line added convertibles and hardtops for '63. Jaunty bucket-seaters like this one were S-22s; bench-seat models came as Customs.* **5.** *Comet again listed two- and four-door wagons for '63. This four-door Custom was the most popular offering, yet sales came to just 5151. A larger 170-cid six became standard for Comet wagons at mid-model year.* **6.** *Meteor engine choices consisted of two sixes and two small V-8s. The $2428 Custom four-door sedan was the Meteor sales leader, at 14,489 units. All models benefited from a number of underskin changes, but the Meteor somehow never found the sales success of sister Ford Fairlane, leading Mercury to try a new approach for '64.*

1. Many critics felt the full-sized Fords hit a new peak with the '64 models. The crisp new styling looked especially fabulous on Galaxie 500 XL two-door hardtops, as seen here. **2.** The popularity of "slantback" hardtops prompted a "faster" roofline for '64 big-Ford sedans, ousting the more formal Thunderbird-type style. Pictured here is the $2678 Galaxie 500 four-door sedan. **3.** The six-passenger Country Sedan was the most popular wagon, with 68,578 sold. **4.** Thunderbird was again all-new for '64, with somewhat more conventional looks. Two hardtops were offered: a base $4486 version and this $4589 Landau with the customary dummy S-bars of the rear quarters of a vinyl-covered roof. **5.** Thunderbird enjoyed record model year sales of 92,465 units, thus eclipsing the 1960 mark at last. T-Bird convertibles started at $4953.

1-2. Ford's milestone Mustang was unveiled at the New York World's Fair in April 1964. Prices as low as $2372 for the hardtop and $2614 for a convertible, plus a plethora of "personal" options, helped make it an instant hit. Its long-hood/short-deck proportions and sporty looks gave birth to a new breed of compacts, nicknamed "ponycars" after the Mustang's equestrian logo. *3.* The midsize Fairlane entered its third season with another facelift. The ferocious Fairlane Thunderbolt was purpose-built for drag racing competition, with a "high-riser" 427 that put out almost 500 hp. *4.* The 500 four-door sedan remained the most popular Fairlane, drawing close to 87,000 sales. *5.* Bucket-seat Fairlane 500 Sport Coupes priced from $2502. *6.* Falcon got its first restyling for '64. Sporty Sprint hardtops and convertibles had a 260 V-8.

1

1. Crafty Texas racer/entrepreneur Carroll Shelby made sports car history when he combined Ford's 260 V-8 with the British A.C. Ace roadster to create the lightning-quick Shelby Cobra. Later production models like this one stepped up to Ford's 271-horse-power 289. **2.** Though it seemed little-changed at first glance, the Lincoln Continental rode a three-inch-longer wheelbase for '64. It also exchanged curved side windows for flat glass. The four-door sedan gained a wider rear window, as seen here. Lincoln sales improved 16 percent to 36,297. **3.** Lincoln Continental kept its classic looks for '64, but the slight upsizing made for a roomier back seat and longer doors for accessing it. Trunks were more spacious, too. Designers kept changing grille treatments, opting this year for a convex vertical-bar affair. Convertible sedan prices started at $6938.

2

3

1

2

3

1. Mercury celebrated its 25th birthday while recalling the past with a reorganized big-car line reviving the Montclair and Park Lane names. Montclair was the middle series, above Monterey, and included this $3127 Marauder "slantback" hardtop. 2. More than 8700 Montclair hardtops came off the assembly line for '64, but 6459 of them were Marauder types. Of that group, just 42 came equipped with the top engine choice, a 425-hp V-8 displacing 427 cubic inches. The big mill, which debuted during the 1963 season, was fed through two big four-barrel carburetors atop an aluminum manifold. 3. For as little as $3116–the cost of a Breezeway four-door sedan–a buyer could drive off with a Montclair. Oblong taillights in place of round units were a subtle rear styling update for '64. 4. The compact Comet was restyled for double duty as the "midsized" Mercury, replacing the Fairlane-based Meteor. Front-fender "ports" were a curious crib from Buick, but Comet sales improved to nearly 190,000, the highest since '61. This "202" two-door sedan was the most affordable model, priced from $2126.

4

SCORECARD 1964		
MAKE	TOTAL PRODUCTION	MKT POSITION
FORD	1,594,053 ▲	2nd ●
LINCOLN	36,297 ▲	13th ●
MERCURY	298,609 ▼	9th ●

1. Full-sized Fords were virtually clean-sheet new for '65, with a new-design frame with wider tracks, revised suspension, and side-rail "torque boxes" that damped out noise and harshness. **2.** Its sleek, semifastback roofline gave the 500XL coupe a slippery profile on the street, and made it the body style of choice for Ford's stock car racing program. **3.** The nicely creased sheetmetal and formal roofline looked sharp on the Galaxie 500 four-door sedan–the sales stalwart among the big Fords. The '65 edition sold 181,183 units, at an MSRP of $2678. **4.** Ford's low-line big cars were still popular with the fleet market and value-conscious retail buyers. This year's offerings comprised two- and four-door sedans in Custom and slightly nicer Custom 500 versions. This Custom two-door was the most affordable big Ford, with a starting price of $2313. **5.** Topping the luxury end of the full-size line was the Galaxie 500 LTD in hardtop coupe or hardtop sedan forms. Vinyl tops were standard on both.

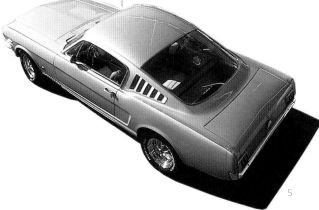

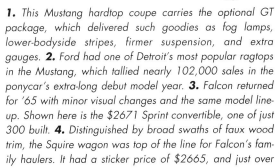

1. This Mustang hardtop coupe carries the optional GT package, which delivered such goodies as fog lamps, lower-bodyside stripes, firmer suspension, and extra gauges. **2.** Ford had one of Detroit's most popular ragtops in the Mustang, which tallied nearly 102,000 sales in the ponycar's extra-long debut model year. **3.** Falcon returned for '65 with minor visual changes and the same model line-up. Shown here is the $2671 Sprint convertible, one of just 300 built. **4.** Distinguished by broad swaths of faux wood trim, the Squire wagon was top of the line for Falcon's family haulers. It had a sticker price of $2665, and just over

6700 were built. **5.** A jaunty fastback coupe arrived for the formal 1965 season to give Mustang buyers a third body choice. **6.** Fairlanes got a somewhat busier look for '65, with knife-edge fenderlines and prominent bodyside creases à la this year's redesigned full-sized Fords. This

500 hardtop coupe was the second most popular '65 Fairlane with 41,405 sales versus 77,000-plus for the 500 four-door sedan. **7.** Station wagons in Ford's family of intermediates again came in base form and as a ritzier Fairlane 500 (shown).

1. Thunderbird's big news for '65 was adoption of standard power front-disc brakes, which resisted fade and water better than drum brakes–important in a two-ton luxury cruiser. 2. T-Bird sales dropped 19 percent for model-year '65 to just under 75,000. At midyear, the base and Landau hardtops were joined by this ritzy $4639 Limited Edition Special Landau, which was purposely limited to just 4500 copies. 3. This Thunderbird convertible, which priced from $4953, wears the dealer-installed "Sport Tonneau" rear-seat cover inspired by the late Sports Roadster model. 4. Lincoln Continental retained its classic styling for '65, with a horizontal theme grille the most obvious change. 5-6. Lincoln sales improved once again, topping 40,000 for the model year. The convertible sedan (shown) carried a $6938 original base price, and accounted for 3356 sales.

1

2

3

Why we drove these beautiful
Comets from Cape Horn to Fairbanks | in 40 days and 40 nights

Because we wanted to show you that | desert, jungle, ice and snow...from | FREE! An exciting, 16-page, full-
Comet's packed with stamina—and | the bottom to the top of the world. | color booklet covering Comet's run
hot performance. That's why! Last | The result: any shorter drive will be | through 14 fascinating countries.
year, specially equipped Comets be- | a picnic with Comet. Try it and see! | Ask your nearby Mercury dealer.
came the World's 100,000-Mile
Durability Champion at Daytona.
Now our regular production '65 has
demonstrated it's just as tough . . .
through 16,200 miles of mountain,

Mercury Comet
the world's 100,000-mile durability

4

1. All Comets got a fresh look for '65, with vertical quad headlights and somewhat busy side sculpturing. This swanky Caliente hardtop coupe started at $2403. 2. Again Mercury's hottest compact, the Comet Cyclone hardtop coupe offered up to 225 hp and a $2683 starting price. 3. The $3511 Colony Park nine-passenger model remained the flagship of Mercury's wagon lineup. 4. Mercury still pushed "Breezeway" styling in '65, but only with four-door sedans. Here, Henry Ford II poses with a top-line Park Lane. A protruding center section and bladelike fender edges help the '65 Mercury acquire some of the Lincoln look up front.

5. Montereys like this hardtop coupe remained the most affordable full-sized Mercs. Prices started at $2902—not including the vinyl top.

5

SCORECARD 1965		
MAKE	TOTAL PRODUCTION	MKT POSITION
FORD	2,170,795 ▲	2nd ●
LINCOLN	40,180 ▲	12th ▲
MERCURY	346,751 ▲	9th ●

1

2

3

4

1. This LTD-based "stretch" limousine was briefly available by special order in 1966. A contract coachbuilder carried out the conversion, but Ford's normal new-car warranty applied. **2.** Galaxie 500 hardtop coupes, with their graceful rooflines and uncluttered styling, were especially handsome full-sized cars. **3.** Returning from 1965 as the finest full-size Ford, the posh Galaxie 500 LTD continued as a hardtop coupe and this hardtop sedan. **4.** Being all-new the previous year, full-sized Fords got mainly minor refinements for '66. Wagons, including this Country Squire, got a "Magic Doorgate" that could be dropped down like a tailgate or swung open like a door. **5.** Ford's midsize Fairlane was overhauled for '66 with smooth new styling on wider bodies that allowed room for big-block V-8s. Ford built 57 dragstrip-ready Fairlanes with 425-horsepower 427 V-8s and lift-off fiberglass hoods. **6.** With 75,947 built, the Fairlane 500 hardtop was the most popular model in the '66 Fairlane lineup.

5

6

1. A convertible body style was a new addition to the Fairlane lineup. This Vintage Burgundy example wears 500/XL trim and is equipped with Fairlane's base V-8, the 200-hp 289. Fairlane GTs and GT/As got a 335-hp 390. **2.** The '66 Falcon was a much-changed compact, becoming a shorter version of the new midsize Fairlane. Models were pared to base and Futura sedans and four-door wagons. This Futura Sports Coupe was the most interesting, with its bucket-seat interior and top-line trim, but sales were modest at 20,089. Total Falcon sales dropped below 183,000. **3.** Mustang got only detail updates for '66, plus base prices hiked slightly, but sales kept galloping: a hearty 607,568 for the normal 12-month selling season. Other manufacturers were scrambling to bring competitive models to market. **4.** The 2+2 fastback remained the least popular Mustang, drawing 35,698 sales versus nearly 500,000 hardtops. This example is equipped with the popular GT package and styled steel wheels. **5.** The small front fender badge indicates that this Mustang convertible is 289 V-8 powered. The base engine remained a 200-cid six.

1. Thunderbirds were gilded a bit for '66, gaining a new face and full-width taillights. The Landau (shown) also got a wide quarter roofline, as did a new lower-cost Town Hardtop that did without a vinyl roof. **2.** At $4426 to start, the hardtop coupe was the most affordable '66 Thunderbird. **3.** The fourth-generation T-Bird bowed out after '66. So did the ragtop after just 5049 sales. A torquey 345-hp 428-cid V-8 was now optional for all T-Birds, but total sales fell again, this time to 69,176. **4.** A Sports Roadster-style tonneau was still available, but rarely ordered. **5.** Lincoln Continental was restyled for 1966, but kept its "classic" character. A projected hood and central grille section implied more power, and a new 462-cid V-8 delivered 20 ponies more than the previous 430—340 in all. A big factor in Lincoln's '66 sales upsurge was the return of a hardtop coupe model after six years. Priced $265 below the four-door at $5485, it drew respectable sales of 15,766. **6.** Continental convertibles gained a glass rear window, but declined in popularity, with just 3180 made.

1. Full-size '66 Mercurys received several refinements to their year-old basic design, including a new 330-hp 410 V-8 as standard for top-line Park Lanes like this $3387 hardtop coupe. Sales were down throughout Detroit after a record '65, and the senior Mercury line shared the retreat, dropping to just under 173,000. **2.** The Park Lane convertible (shown) again topped Mercury's prestige line for '66, starting at $3608. Sales remained modest, with only 2546 being sold. Monterey convertibles priced from $3237 and saw 3279 sales. A new "Stereo-Sonic Tape System," more commonly known as an eight-track cartridge tape player, was available for all big Mercurys. **3-4.** After two years as Mercury's "midsize," Comet literally grew into the role for '66 by becoming a twin to Ford's Fairlane. The performance-oriented Comet Cyclone expanded into a new model line offering coupes and convertibles in base or racy GT trim. Cyclone GTs (shown here) had a 335-horsepower 390 V-8, and could get a four-speed manual transmission.

FORD

1. Full-sized '67 Fords kept their existing wheelbases, but adopted flowing lines that added three inches to overall length. The woody-look Country Squire priced from $3234. 2. Hardtop coupes, such as the $2755 Galaxie 500, gained a smoother roofline. 3. Thunderbird was clean-sheet fresh for '67, becoming larger and more luxurious than ever. The convertible was gone, but base and Landau hardtops returned, the latter shown here. But the biggest news was a Landau four-door sedan on a 2.5-inch-longer wheelbase.

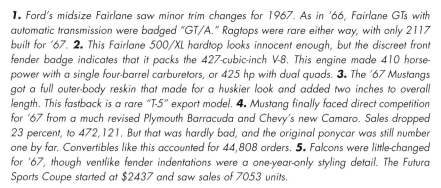

1. Ford's midsize Fairlane saw minor trim changes for 1967. As in '66, Fairlane GTs with automatic transmission were badged "GT/A." Ragtops were rare either way, with only 2117 built for '67. **2.** This Fairlane 500/XL hardtop looks innocent enough, but the discreet front fender badge indicates that it packs the 427-cubic-inch V-8. This engine made 410 horsepower with a single four-barrel carburetors, or 425 hp with dual quads. **3.** The '67 Mustangs got a full outer-body reskin that made for a huskier look and added two inches to overall length. This fastback is a rare "T-5" export model. **4.** Mustang finally faced direct competition for '67 from a much revised Plymouth Barracuda and Chevy's new Camaro. Sales dropped 23 percent, to 472,121. But that was hardly bad, and the original ponycar was still number one by far. Convertibles like this accounted for 44,808 orders. **5.** Falcons were little-changed for '67, though ventlike fender indentations were a one-year-only styling detail. The Futura Sports Coupe started at $2437 and saw sales of 7053 units.

1. U.S. Shelby Cobra sales ended in '67 due to forth-coming safety regulations. By this time, Carroll Shelby was building updated "427" roadsters with big-block Ford V-8s that could be tweaked to 480 horsepower. Cobra 427s were built from 1965-1967 with more muscular "wide body" styling than the small-block cars first made in 1962. All Cobras had too much power for their chassis, but 427s were truly scary–and unforgettable. 2. Lincoln Continental returned from its '66 redesign with minimal exterior change. Inside, though, all models boasted a new "Fresh Flow" ventilation system that forced air from the dashboard vents through extractors concealed in a low-pressure area at the rear. Hardtop coupes started at $5553 compared to $5795 for the four-door sedan and $6449 for the four-door ragtop, America's only convertible sedan. 3. Lincoln sales retreated to 45,667 for '67. Demand for the unique four-door open Continental, which had been waning from its high point in 1965, slipped to 2276 units. With that, Dearborn accountants decided they could no longer afford continuing the model, so this was its last year. But with yearly production always so modest, all Lincoln convertibles of the Sixties have since become prized collector cars. They're also sought after for their clean, classic styling.

1. Mercury joined the ponycar craze with the '67 Cougar, a nicely restyled Mustang hardtop with a three-inch-longer wheelbase and a greater luxury emphasis. Hidden head-lamps and a 289 V-8 were standard for this $2851 base model and the upscale XR-7, whose $3081 starting price included leather seat surfaces, woodgrain dash appliqué, and full instrumentation. **2.** The Cougar attracted 150,893 customers in its debut year. Slick sequential rear turn signals were a standard feature. **3.** The unchanged Comet roster for '67 was again headed by the Cyclone with GT equipment. A new full-width, single-element grille was employed (with blacked-out sections on Cyclones). The GT hardtop now began at $3034, a $143 increase over the previous year. **4.** A "mod" paisley vinyl roof was a pro-posed Cougar option, but didn't make the catalog. **5.** Full-sized '67 Mercurys sported a Lincoln-like bulged nose, but weren't greatly changed. This Monterey S-55 two-door hardtop is one of just 570 produced.

SCORECARD 1967		
MAKE	TOTAL PRODUCTION	MKT POSITION
FORD	1,730,224 ▾	2nd ▾
LINCOLN	45,667 ▾	12th •
MERCURY	354,923 ▴	8th •

1. Replacing the 427 as a special-order Mustang option, the muscular ram air Cobra Jet arrived in time for the winter 1967-1968 pro drag races. This modified fastback won a class trophy for owner/driver Al Joniec at the NHRA Winternationals in Pomona, California, after a quarter-mile run of 12.5 seconds at 97.93 mph. **2.** Mustang cantered

into '68 with no basic design changes, but sales dipped 32 percent. This well-kept GT is one of 249,447 hardtops built for the model year, which was nearly 107,000 down on the '67 run. This car's distinctive "C-stripes" were a new appearance item separate from the GT option, and proved fairly popular. **3.** Vinyl roof, whitewalls, and wire wheel

covers remained popular 1968 dress-up options for basic six-cylinder Mustangs like this hardtop. Also note the new-for-'68 side-marker lights, which were now required by federal safety regulations. **4-5.** Carroll Shelby's Mustangs returned for '68 with a fastback and convertible in small-block GT-350 guise and big-inch GT-500 trim. At midyear, the 500s added the initials KR–for "King of the Road"–and exchanged a 390-cubic-inch V-8 for a new Ford 428. Both engines were advertised at 335 horsepower, but the 428 produced more like 400 actual horsepower. Though Shelby Mustangs still looked wilder than Ford's ponies, they were fast becoming less special. The $4117 GT-350 fastback was the year's popularity champ, with 1253 sold. Output of GT-500 convertibles was a mere 402 units.

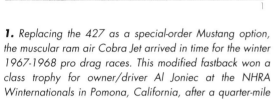

1. *Thunderbirds showed an eggcrate grille pattern and other cosmetic tweaks for '68. Shown here is the $4924 Landau sedan.* 2. *All big Fords again wore new lower-body sheetmetal. This rakish Galaxie 500 XL fastback hardtop coupe shared a new hidden-headlamp face with the year's XL ragtop, all LTDs, and the Country Squire wagon.* 3. *Clean-sheet bodies with more flowing lines highlighted 1968's midsized Fords. Fairlane was downplayed in favor of related but flashier new Torinos, which formed a separate series. Shown here is the $2688 Torino four-door sedan.* 4. *The $3032 Torino Squire wagon topped Ford's new upmarket midsize line.* 5. *Replacing Fairlane GTs for '68 was a trio of Torino GTs: convertible, hardtop coupe, and this racy new fastback.* 6. *This Futura four-door sedan shows off Falcon's new-for-'68 squarish taillights and side-marker lamps.* 7. *The Torino GT ragtop was chosen pace car for the 1968 Indianapolis 500.* 8. *At $2728 to start, the Futura wagon was the costliest Falcon. Unlike some other compacts, Falcon returned to its roots after '65, emphasizing high value and economy.*

1. A better Lincoln idea bowed in April 1968 with the Continental Mark III, a $6585 hardtop coupe built on the four-door T-Bird chassis. Chairman Henry Ford II saw it picking up from the 1956-1957 Continental Mark II, so the new car had a humped decklid and long-hood/short-deck proportions. Though hardly cheap, the Mark III offered power everything, an ultraluxurious interior with extra noise insulation, numerous color choices, and a 460 V-8. Initial sales were encouraging, at 7770 units. **2.** The 1968 Lincoln Continental hardtop received a revised roofline with wider, more "formal" rear quarters. The model priced from $5736. Its four-door sister was $234 more. Sales for these Lincolns slipped to 39,134, the lowest level since 1964. Relative year-to-year sameness didn't help, but the main factor was the late-1967 auto workers strike that cut into the production of most Ford Motor Company products. **3.** Lincoln Continentals lost their stand-up hood ornament for '68 due to new federal safety rules, but it would be back. Meantime, the "star" logo moved down the nose above a new thin-bar grille. A 365-hp 460-cid V-8 replaced the 462 V-8 as a running change. A four-door sedan like this marked production of the one-millionth Lincoln on March 25, 1968.

1

2

3

1. This '68 Mercury Park Lane convertible sports wagonlike "Yacht Paneling" bodyside trim, which arrived as a midyear option. **2.** A new face moved full-sized '68 Mercurys even closer to Lincoln in appearance. This hardtop sedan was once used in the long-running Hawaii Five-O television series. **3.** The Mercury Marquis hardtop coupe returned for '68 solely as a hardtop coupe with its own formal roofline. **4.** Midsized Mercs for '68 comprised sporty Cyclones and new luxury-minded Montegos. Here, the Montego MX hardtop coupe. **5.** Of the 13,638 Cyclones built this model year, just 334 were GT notchbacks like the one seen here. GT fastbacks saw sales of 6105. **6.** The rare Cougar XR-7G included a special hood scoop and power sunroof. The "G" stood for racing legend Dan Gurney.

SCORECARD 1968

MAKE	TOTAL PRODUCTION	MKT POSITION
FORD	1,753,334 ▲	2nd ●
LINCOLN	46,904 ▲	12th ●
MERCURY	360,467 ▲	8th ●

1. A stem-to-stern redesign made '69 Mustangs longer, lower, wider, a bit heavier, and much swoopier. The Boss 302 was a street version of Ford's all-out Trans-Am racer. Its small-block V-8 was rated at 290 horsepower. **2.** The '69 Shelbys were the tamest yet, just regular Mustangs with a specific big-mouth fiberglass front, scoops and scallops all over, and wide taillamps. This ragtop GT-500 is one of just 335 built. **3.** Reflecting a snowballing market trend, Mustang convertible sales dropped for '69, despite the ponycar's redesign and a base price hiked just $35 to $2849. Model-year volume plunged 42 percent to 14,746. **4.** Even with aggressive new styling, Mustangs retained signature ponycar cues and proportions for '69. The racy new Mach 1 fastback featured handling suspension, upsized wheels and tires, and unique exterior trim. Ford's new 351-cid V-8 was standard, but the potent 428 Cobra Jet was optional. So was a novel "shaker" hood scoop. **5.** The Boss 429 was ready-made for the dragstrip and enabled Ford to qualify an exotic new "semi-hemi" V-8 for stock car racing. The Mustang's compact engine bay and chassis required several modifications before the gargantuan 429-cid big block would fit. **6.** Nineteen sixty-nine Thunderbirds displayed minor trim changes and a revived sliding metal sunroof option. To Ford's dismay, sales plummeted to 49,272, the lowest model-year tally since 1958.

1. The big '69 Fords were rebodied on a new 121-inch wheel-base chassis, up two inches from 1960-68. Length grew two to three inches, and width and weight increased. The pseudo-wood-sided Country Squire continued as Ford's luxury wagon flagship. 2. Ford's '69 big-car redesign brought a racy "tunnelback" roofline to the Galaxie 500 hardtop coupe and its XL sister (shown). The rear window sat between "flying buttress" pillars that gave a fastback profile. 3. The XL convertible and hardtop coupe remained the sportiest big-Ford models. XL ragtops were rare; this is one of a handful packing a big 429-cubic-inch V-8 with "ram air" hood scoop. Sales of '69 full-sized Fords topped the one-million mark. 4-5. Answering Plymouth's "budget muscle" Road Runner, the '69 Torino Cobra fastback SportRoof (left) and notchback hardtop delivered a 335-horsepower 428-cid Cobra Jet V-8–and 0-60 mph in just six seconds–for less than $3200.

1

2

3

4

1. Lincoln Continentals received another round of considerable refinements for '69, plus exterior changes including a grille that looked cribbed from snooty Mercedes-Benz—perhaps not unintended. Chicago's Lehmann-Peterson works was still building some 50-60 stretched "Executive Sedan" limousines like this a year. **2.** Lincoln Continental sales had another setback for '69, slipping to about 38,300. As ever, the sedan took the lion's share. This year it priced from $6063 versus $5830 for the hardtop coupe (shown), which found 9032 buyers. Exclusive to the sedan was a new "Town Car" interior option with "super puff" leather/vinyl upholstery and "extra plush" carpeting. All '69 Lincolns continued to use the 460-cid V-8 engine that provided 365 hp. **3-4.** Mercury matched Ford's new Torino Cobra with its own "budget muscle" midsize, the Cyclone CJ. The initials, of course, stood for Cobra Jet, as in a standard 335-hp 428 V-8. The CJ came only in fastback form and, as expected of a Mercury, cost a bit more than the Ford: $3224 to start. With just 3261 built, the Cyclone CJ is scarce today. **5.** Mercury honored two of its NASCAR drivers with namesake Cyclone Spoilers. The red/white "Cale Yarborough Special" was sold by western dealers, while the blue/white "Dan Gurney Special" was sold in the east. About 300 were produced as the Spoiler II (shown), with the elongated nose and blacked-out grille borrowed from the Ford Torino Talledega.

5

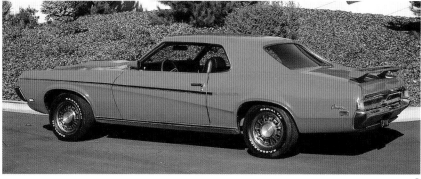

1-2. After just two years on the market, the Cougar was revamped along the same lines as the '69 Mustang. The top performance model was the striped, spoilered, and scooped Eliminator, which came standard with a 290-horsepower 351. Big-block 428s were optional. **3.** Cougar styling was reinterpreted, with sweeping Buick-like creaselines on the bodysides. This XR-7 hardtop, one of 23,918 built, priced from $3315. **4-5.** Sporty Mercury Marauder X-100 hardtop coupes included a standard 360-hp 429 V-8 and styled aluminum wheels. They shared a "tunnelback" roofline with Ford's big XL hardtop, but rear fender skirts and a matte-black decklid were unique to the Merc. The X-100 drew 5635 sales.

SCORECARD **1969**		
MAKE	TOTAL PRODUCTION	MKT POSITION
FORD	1,826,777 ▲	2nd ●
LINCOLN	61,378 ▲	12th ●
MERCURY	398,262 ▲	8th ●

GENERAL MOTORS CORPORATION

Someone once said that General Motors was so large it could be mismanaged for 10 years before anyone would notice. Though GM would struggle in later decades, it did very little wrong in the 1960s, cruising on as the biggest in the business, if not always the best.

As it had in the Fifties, GM owned some 40-50 percent of the U.S. new-car market, dominance almost unimaginable nowadays. Four of its five nameplates were consistent top-10 sellers. In a total market of some 7.5-9.5 million sales per year, Chevrolet alone typically drew around two million. Pontiac passed American Motors after 1961 to claim a solid number three, right behind Ford. Buick and Oldsmobile always outpaced rivals in the medium-price field, and GM's flagship Cadillac Division remained America's luxury leader by far, outselling archrival Lincoln by at least two-to-one.

Sheer size explains much of this success. It insulated GM from market shifts that competitors couldn't weather as well. Size also allowed GM to attract a deeper, broader pool of design, engineering, and marketing talent. And even on the rare occasion when it was caught by surprise, as with Ford's Falcon compact and Mustang "ponycar," GM was quick to recover.

GM also continued to innovate in the Sixties, mainly because it could afford to dare most anything it wished. Not all these efforts were consumer home runs, but most were. Enthusiasts have long recognized the excellence of the 1963 Buick Riviera, Chevrolet Corvette Sting Ray, and Pontiac Grand Prix; the '64 Pontiac GTO, the original "muscle car"; and the 1966 Oldsmobile Toronado and '67 Cadillac Eldorado, the most ambitious, powerful front-wheel-drive cars ever built—to name but a few. GM also showed an uncanny knack for making good on "mistakes," transforming the Chevrolet Corvair, for example, from oddball econocar to sporty "driver's" machine that actually provided the rationale for the phenomenally successful Mustang.

Even so, the original 1960-64 Corvair was GM's biggest mistake of the decade, thanks to some cost-conscious engineering that roused the ire of a young attorney named Ralph Nader. It was his damning book on that car, *Unsafe at Any Speed*, that spurred Washington to enact the first in a long line of safety standards that would forever change the auto business, starting with model-year 1968. GM unwisely added fuel to the fire by hiring private investigators in an effort to discredit Nader, all to no avail.

Yet even if absolute power corrupts, as it so often does, General Motors in the 1960s produced many cars that a great many people wanted to buy, and which still stand as exemplars of the age. Nader notwithstanding, this was the last truly uneventful decade for a company that remains a symbol of everything right—and wrong—with American business.

1-2. *Like other General Motors cars of 1960, Buicks were toned-down versions of the all-new 1959 models, though Buick's basic "delta wing" design was still pretty wild. The facelift did revive Buick's trademark: front fender "ventiports." Top-line Electras and Electra 225s had four of the decorative accents, versus three for midrange Invictas and entry-level LeSabres. The '60s also wore a prominent new "tri-shield" Buick logo. The Electra hardtop sedan (above) priced from $3963, $337 less than its Electra 225 sibling (below). The extra money bought extra length; Electra 225s were 225.9 inches long overall, more than four inches longer than regular Electras.*

1. Buick's best-selling convertible for 1960 was the LeSabre, which reached a production level of 13,588 units. Perhaps that's not surprising, because at $3145 it was $1047 less than the Electra 225 ragtop. 2. The 1960 Buicks' voluptuous curves made even the station wagons look swoopy. Invicta Estate Wagons started at $3841 with two-row seating, or $3948 with a rearward-facing third-row seat. 3. Cadillac ruled the luxury roost as the 1960s dawned, outselling Lincoln, Chrysler, and Imperial combined. This stately Series 75 limousine is one of just 832 produced. The price was an equally stately $9748.

1-2. Cadillac's 1959 styling was the height of Fifties flamboyance. Designers dialed back for the new decade, making the 1960 models more restrained, with lower tailfins and less gaudy grilles immediately evident. Convertibles, as always, were the glamour leaders, comprising a mainstream Series 62 model and the limited-edition Eldorado Biarritz (shown). With 1285 produced, the Biarritz was the best-selling Eldorado. **3.** The Biarritz's hardtop sibling, the $7401 Seville coupe, rounded out the Eldorado line along with an ultralimited Brougham hardtop sedan. All Eldorados used 390-cubic-inch V-8s like other models, but had a three two-barrel carburetor setup that netted 345 horsepower versus 325.

1-2. Detroit's Big Three debuted compact cars for 1960. Chevy's Corvair was the most radical by far. Instead of a water-cooled engine in front, Corvair used a unique air-cooled "flat" six-cylinder placed at the rear. Corvair bowed in coupe and four-door sedan models in plain 500 and slightly ritzier 700 trim. A full perimeter chrome strip identified 700s like this four-door sedan, which carried a starting price of $2103. **3.** Corvair model-year sales totaled just over 250,000. Of those, 36,562 were 700 club coupes like this one. **4.** The 1960 Corvette looked identical to the '59, but model-year volume set a record at 10,261. Engines were unchanged, but the suspension gained a rear sway bar and other revisions.

1-2. *Perennial sales leader Chevrolet was in the second—and final—year of its "bat-wing" tail styling for passenger cars. Pictured are the ritziest models in the full-size lineup, the $2954 Impala convertible and the $2704 Impala Sport Coupe hardtop.* **3.** *Nomad remained Chevy's most luxurious wagon for 1960. It was again offered only as a six-passenger four-door with Impala-level trim and equipment.* **4.** *Oldsmobile pried the tinsel off its all-new 1959s to create one of 1960's more attractive cars. Offerings again spanned Dynamic 88s, Super 88s, and top-line Ninety-Eights. Here, the Super 88 ragtop.* **5.** *Ninety-Eights rode an exclusive 126.3-inch wheelbase, versus 123 for the others. Dealers saw sales fall 10 percent in a compact-minded market.*

1

3

2

4

5

1

1. The 1960 Pontiacs sold even better than the all-new '59s on which they were based. Fresh styling and new colors aided the cause. All '60 Pontiacs used a 389-cubic-inch V-8, which ranged from an economical 215 horsepower to 348 on Tri-Power Bonnevilles. The Star Chief two-door sedan made its final appearance for 1960. Just 5757 were made. 2. The Vista Sedan four-door hardtop, a body style that debuted for 1959, was again the most popular Bonneville for '60, with 39,037 sold. Its unique wraparound rear window design was shared with other GM four-door hardtops. 3. Priciest 1960 Pontiac was the Bonneville Custom Safari station wagon, which started at $3530. 4. Pontiac again promoted the handling virtues of its "Wide Track" design, a marketing gem that also enhanced the appearance of its cars.

2

3

4

SCORECARD 1960		
MAKE	TOTAL PRODUCTION	MKT POSITION
BUICK	253,807 ▼	9th ▼
CADILLAC	142,184 ▼	10th •
CHEVROLET	1,653,168 ▲	1st •
OLDSMOBILE	347,142 ▼	7th ▼
PONTIAC	396,716 ▲	5th ▼

GENERAL MOTORS

1

2

3

4

5

6

7

Cadillac individuality
The Cadillac car is offered in such an abundance of choices that it would take ten years of continuous production to create every possible Cadillac combination.

8

9

1-2. The 1961 Buicks were fully redesigned with much cleaner "bullet-nose" styling. Most affordable droptop was the $3382 LeSabre convertible. The bigger and flashier Electra 225 convertible started at $4192. **3.** The '61 Buicks' crisply sculpted bodyside coves lent themselves to two-tone paint, as shown on this Invicta two-door hardtop. **4-5.** At first glance, the Electra two-door hardtop (left) looks identical to its LeSabre sibling, but a closer look reveals four "portholes" versus two, a more-straight-edged hardtop roofline shared with Cadillac and the Oldsmobile Ninety Eight, and a longer wheelbase (126 inches versus 123). Under the hood, LeSabre made do with a 364-cid V-8 while other full-size Buicks came standard with a 401 V-8. **6.** Buick joined the compact-car stampede with the Special. It bowed in two- and four-door sedan and four-door wagon body styles priced between $2330 and $2816. **7.** Introduced at midyear, the Skylark was a sporty Special coupe with a distinct grille and taillamp treatment, a vinyl top, and a 185-hp version of the 215 V-8. **8.** Cadillac was all-new for '61, shedding a few inches and pounds while gaining a crisp, chiseled look. Highlighting the new design were lower-body "skeg fins" and arched windshield posts—no more Fifties-faddish "doglegs" to bang knees. Regaining its flagship status with the demise of the Eldorado Brougham was the Series 60 Special, a formal-roof hardtop costing $6233. **9.** Two-door hardtops came either as this Coupe de Ville, starting at $5252, or as the Series 62, beginning at $4892. At the rear, oval pods held taillamps and backup lights. Cadillac's sole engine was again a 390-cid V-8, though now it came only as a 325-hp four-barrel.

1. Along with their corporate sisters, Chevy's 1961 "standards" were the first General Motors cars to bear the full imprint of corporate design chief Bill Mitchell. The result was a cleaner, more coherent big Chevy that was 1.5 inches shorter yet looked much trimmer despite an unchanged 119-inch wheelbase. This gorgeous Impala Sport Coupe wears the optional Super Sport package that was a midyear addition along with the soon to be legendary 409 V-8. 2. As in recent years, full-sized Chevy wagons had their own names for 1961, though still outfitted in parallel with the three non-wagon series. The Impala-level four-door Nomad remained top of the line, but a nine-passenger version joined the six-seat model this year. Nomad prices started at $2996 with base V-8. 3-4. A bucket-seater Monza coupe was a late-1960 model-year addition to the Corvair line. A four-door-sedan body style (left) joined the Corvair Monza roster for '61, but the Monza coupe was the real showroom dynamo, handily outselling every other Corvair. Chevrolet executives took careful note of this seemingly untapped enthusiast market. 5. Corvette received a "taillift" with four round taillights in a "ducktailed" rear end for '61, its first major styling change since 1958. Up front, a simple mesh grill replaced the familiar chrome "teeth." Engines were unchanged, but a 315-hp "fuelie" with a four-speed manual shift could hit 60 mph in 5.5 seconds and top 130 mph. Base price rose to $3934, which may explain why sales rose only fractionally to 10,939, though that was still another Corvette record.

1. Oldsmobile remade its image in '61, shifting from performance to premium-car luxury. Its big cars looked crisper, more mature, and made better use of space. The new flagship of the line was the $4647 Starfire, a deluxe-trimmed convertible intended to compete in the emerging personal-luxury field. Built on the 123-inch Super 88 chassis, Starfires got bucket seats and a console, Ninety-Eight grille, rear panel trim, and a brushed-finish bodyside trim panel. All full-sized '61 Oldsmobiles used a 394-cubic-inch V-8, but the Starfire got an exclusive 330-horsepower version. **2.** The best-selling Super 88 model was the $3402 Holiday hardtop sedan, with an output of 23,272 units. **3.** The aft view shows off handsome rear-end styling, with round taillights set in a sculpted cove and "skeg" fins similar to the '61 Cadillacs'. **4.** The top-line Ninety-Eight series featured two four-door hardtops; the $4021 Holiday hardtop sedan and this $4159 Sport Sedan. Ninety-Eights retained a 126.3-inch span but lost two inches of body length. **5.** Even the cheapest full-size hardtop, the $2956 Dynamic 88 coupe, cut a sharp figure. In all, Oldsmobile built 317,548 cars for '61, a slight drop from '60 in an overall slow car market, but enough to move up a notch to sixth in the industry.

SCORECARD 1961

MAKE	TOTAL PRODUCTION	MKT POSITION
BUICK	276,754 ▼	8th ▲
CADILLAC	138,379 ▼	10th •
CHEVROLET	1,318,014 ▼	2nd ▼
OLDSMOBILE	317,548 ▼	6th ▲
PONTIAC	340,635 ▼	5th •

1-2. Pontiac's compact Tempest debuted for '61 as a four-door sedan (shown) and station wagon, with a choice of standard or optional Custom interior trim. A coupe body style followed later in the model year. Standard power came from a 195-cid four-cylinder engine derived from a bank of Pontiac's 389-cube V-8; a 215-cid V-8 was optional. Both engines were linked to a very unconventional drivetrain: a flexible-cable driveshaft connected to a rear transaxle. Front suspension was independent of course, and swing axles made the rear independent,

too. **3.** Pontiac's redesigned fleet of big cars revived the split-grille theme on shorter and lower but roomier bodies. Two-door hardtops, like this $2971 Ventura, shared the new "bubble roof" with Chevy and Olds. Optional eight-lug aluminum rims, exclusive to Pontiac, combined wheel hub and brake drum. All big Pontiacs used the 389-cid V-8, which could be ordered with as much as 348 horsepower. Late in the year, the 373-hp special-order Super Duty 421 debuted. **4.** Top-line Bonnevilles, like this $3331 Vista Sedan four-door hardtop, got ritzier trim with flashy triple taillamps. The track width of the full-sized '61 Pontiacs was reduced by 1½ inches, but that didn't dent the "wide-track" advertising slogan.

GENERAL MOTORS

Special Announcement for 1962... No words, no pictures, no cute little tune can give you the whole great story of the 1962 Buick Special. You must get behind the wheel, drive the car, then listen to your head and your heart—that's the story. Meanwhile, here are some facts: 1. There's a new Buick Special convertible for 1962, as dashing and sprightly a car as you ever saw. 2. For '62 the Buick Special brings you a great new exclusive—the new V-6 engine. Perfect mating of the vim and vigor of V-design with the economy of a six. Great running mate for the famous Buick Special aluminum V-8. 3. Your choice of Dual-Path automatic transmission or a new 4-speed "stick shift" synchromesh? 4. New trims, new colors, eight new models to choose from—*every one a Buick through and through.* 5. The lilt of Skylark styling, inspired by Buick's great sports-minded fun car. Do something Special for yourself. Drive America's *happy-medium size car—* **Buick Special '62**

1

3

4

5

2

6

7

8

1. Big Buicks were restyled for 1962, but compact Specials retained the pointed-fender styling theme from '61. The premium Skylark model expanded from a single two-door pillared coupe to add a geniune two-door hardtop and this flashy convertible. 2. Specials got a notable new standard powerplant: America's first mass-produced passenger-car V-6. The 198-cid engine made 135 horsepower. 3. Electra 225 remained the top-line Buick series. Convertibles began at $4366. 4. Invicta Estate Wagons started at $3917 in nine-passenger form. 5. The "bubbletop" coupe roof of '61 was replaced for '62 by the more upright style seen on this LeSabre two-door hardtop. 6. Among the 16,734 Electra 225 four-door hardtops built for 1962 were some made into long-wheelbase eight-passenger limousines by the Flxible Company of Loudonville, Ohio. 7-9. Cadillacs got subtle styling tweaks for '62, including a revised grille texture, rectangular front parking lights, slightly subdued tailfins, and vertical taillight housings. The Series 62 convertible started at $5588, while the Sedan De Ville priced from $5631.

9

1

2

3

4

5

6

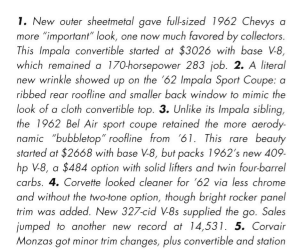

NEW CHEVY II

8

The Saturday Evening Post

Nova 400 Sport Coupe—handsome hardtop with Body by Fisher.

Luxury and low price...beautifully blended

This is just one of 11 frisky, family-sized Chevy II models that have many a bigger car wondering how it's done. You may, too . . . when you see how much perky performance, pert good looks and relaxing roominess you get in one of America's lowest priced cars!

Like a car that fits big families and small parking places? A sassy, saving six with V8 zest? One-piece rear springs for a softer, quieter ride? Money-saving maintenance features like front-end components (including fenders) that bolt on for easy replacement? You'll find them all and then some in Chevy II—the same ingenious things that won Car Life magazine's coveted Engineering Excellence Award. The same day-in, day-out dependability that means any car is a sounder buy if Chevrolet builds it. See for yourself at your dealer's now! . . . Chevrolet Division of General Motors, Detroit 2, Michigan.

Chevy II Nova

CHEVROLET

9

1. New outer sheetmetal gave full-sized 1962 Chevys a more "important" look, one now much favored by collectors. This Impala convertible started at $3026 with base V-8, which remained a 170-horsepower 283 job. **2.** A literal new wrinkle showed up on the '62 Impala Sport Coupe: a ribbed rear roofline and smaller back window to mimic the look of a cloth convertible top. **3.** Unlike its Impala sibling, the 1962 Bel Air sport coupe retained the more aerodynamic "bubbletop" roofline from '61. This rare beauty started at $2668 with base V-8, but packs 1962's new 409-hp V-8, a $484 option with solid lifters and twin four-barrel carbs. **4.** Corvette looked cleaner for '62 via less chrome and without the two-tone option, though bright rocker panel trim was added. New 327-cid V-8s supplied the go. Sales jumped to another new record at 14,531. **5.** Corvair Monzas got minor trim changes, plus convertible and station wagon body styles for '62. Shown here is the four-door sedan, which started at $2273–the same base price as the Monza coupe. **6.** The Corvair Monza Spyder came in coupe or convertible form, both packing a turbocharged version of the 145-cid "flat" six that churned out 150 hp. **7.** Taking over for Corvair as Chevy's mainstream compact, the '62 Chevy II was as simple and conventional as its targeted rival, the successful Ford Falcon. Topping the new line was this snazzy Nova 400 convertible, which saw 23,741 copies. **8-9.** The Chevy II line's only hardtop was the Nova 400 Sport Coupe, of which 59,586 were built for '62. The debut Chevy II way outsold Corvair, but even with 327,000 units, it couldn't beat Ford's still-popular Falcon.

1-2. *Oldsmobile's F-85 compacts debuted for '61. At midyear '62, Olds unveiled the innovative Jetfire, a bucket-seat F-85 coupe that was powered by a turbo-charged 215-cid V-8. Available with manual or automatic transmission, the Jetfire could do 0-60 mph in a credible for the day 8.5 seconds.* **3-4.** *New nose and tail styling for its big cars helped Oldsmobile to its best sales year since 1956. The bucket-seat Starfire became its own series and added a coupe. The $4131 hardtop outsold the convertible—at $4774, the priciest Olds—34,839 to 7149.*

1-2. *Pontiac's new Grand Prix would help define the personal-luxury field. Sales of 30,195 made it a hit. The $3490 base price included bucket seats and a 303-horsepower 389.* **3.** *Nineteen sixty-two was a breakthrough year for Pontiac, when more than a half-million of the division's products were built, including more than 380,000 of the full-sized cars. The biggest Pontiac hardtop coupe was the $3349 Bonneville.* **4.** *The nine-seat Catalina Safari station wagon started at $3301.* **5.** *Flashiest member of the broad Catalina lineup was the $3172 convertible.* **6-7.** *A convertible body style joined the Tempest roster for '62. Also new was a sporty, bucket-seat LeMans option package, available on coupes and droptops (both shown here).*

SCORECARD 1962		
MAKE	TOTAL PRODUCTION	MKT. POSITION
BUICK	399,526 ▲	6th ▲
CADILLAC	160,840 ▲	10th •
CHEVROLET	2,061,677 ▲	1st ▲
OLDSMOBILE	428,853 ▲	5th ▲
PONTIAC	521,933 ▲	3rd ▲

GENERAL MOTORS

1-2. The Buick Riviera was reborn for 1963 as a stunning $4365 hardtop coupe artfully blending American and British style. This svelte personal-luxury car changed Buick's stodgy image almost overnight. **3.** Buick's smallest car, the Special, kept a 112-inch wheelbase but got a new look that included slab bodysides. Top-line Skylarks, like this $2857 Sports Coupe, got a 200-hp 215 V-8. **4.** The $3339 LeSabre convertible was the most affordable and popular big Buick ragtop. **5.** Best-selling Electra 225 was the $4186 four-window hard-top sedan. **6.** Buick's sporty Wildcat was promoted to its own model line. Body styles now included convertible and hardtop coupes, and this $3871 hardtop sedan.

1. Another redesign helped Cadillac to a new sales record of more than 163,000 for '63. The division also reworked its engine for the first time in 14 years, making it lighter, more fuel efficient, smoother, and more reliable. Horsepower was still rated at 325, but Cadillacs shed a few pounds, so performance improved, with 0-60 mph down to only about 10 seconds. Cadillac's best-selling model, at 31,749 units, was this dashing $5386 Coupe DeVille. **2.** Cadillac's marquee car, the Eldorado Biarritz, was facelifted along with the other 1963s and enjoyed the return of its Eldo name in block letters on the front fender. Caddy's other ragtop was in the Series 62 line, but it cost $1018 less than the $6608 Biarritz.

1

2

1-2. Save carryover engines, Corvette was all-new for 1963, gaining Sting Ray badges in a nod to its arresting styling patterned on GM design chief Bill Mitchell's recent Stingray show car. Joining the traditional 'Vette roadster was this sleek fastback coupe with a split rear window that hampered visibility but looked terrific. The coupe helped lift Corvette model-year volume a smashing 48 percent to 21,513 units, accounting for 10,594 of the total. **3.** The '63 Sting Ray convertible started at $4037, versus $4252 for the new coupe. Bodies were still fiberglass, but on a lighter yet stiffer new ladder-type frame with a 98-inch wheelbase, trimmer by four inches. A European-style independent rear suspension replaced the old solid axle for much improved handling. Hidden headlamps were new, and there was no exterior trunklid; cargo access was from inside the cockpit.

3

1. In addition to the Corvette, Chevrolet offered three different convertible lines in '63: the Impala, the Chevy II, and the Corvair Spyder. **2.** Brand-new body designs brought a crisp new look to full-sized '63 Chevrolets. Impala Sport Coupes started at $2774 with the standard 283 V-8. **3.** Side-sculpting gave way to a slab-sided look on '63 Oldsmobiles. Ninety-Eights adopted rear styling all their own; shown here is the $4178 Holiday coupe. **4.** The sporty Olds Starfire again utilized the 88 body, but now wore a distinctively styled hardtop roof. **5.** The $3748 Dynamic 88 wagon was the rarest '63 Olds, with just 3878 sold.

1. Oldsmobile's line changed little, with models still available in three distinct wheelbases. They were, clockwise from top center: the F-85 and Jetfire at 112 inches; Dynamic and Starfire on a 123-inch chassis; and the top-line Ninety-Eight with a 126-inch wheelbase. All offered convertible and hardtop models, and the F-85 and 88 added wagons. 2. Youthful and energetic, Pontiac's 1963 restyle was one of the era's benchmarks. The full-sized models' stacked headlights would be copied by other cars. This Bonneville convertible wears a rare optional fiberglass top. 3-4. The Grand Prix entered its sophomore season wearing handsome new sheetmetal with smooth bodysides, a concave rear window, and "hidden" taillamps. The Pontiac division saw its highest model-year production to date, 590,071, under the leadership of general manager E.M. "Pete" Estes.

1

2

3   4

1-2. The sporty LeMans became a separate Tempest series for '63 with a $2742 convertible and $2418 hardtop coupe. **3.** This Tempest wagon is one of only six originally built for dragstrip competition with Pontiac's ferocious Super Duty 421. **4.** This Catalina two-door hardtop packs a High Output 421 with Tri-Power carburetion and 370 horsepower. **5.** The $3179 convertible was the flashiest member of Pontiac's mainstream Catalina line. Its sales hit 18,249.

SCORECARD 1963

MAKE	TOTAL PRODUCTION	MKT POSITION
BUICK	457,818 ▲	7th ▼
CADILLAC	163,174 ▲	10th ●
CHEVROLET	2,237,201 ▲	1st ●
OLDSMOBILE	476,753 ▲	5th ●
PONTIAC	590,071 ▲	3rd ●

GENERAL MOTORS

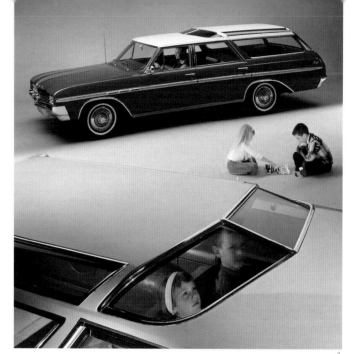

1. Big Buick styling was further refined for 1964. Bright lower bodyside trim and new standard fender skirts accentuated the exclusive 126-inch wheelbase of Electra 225 models. Four-door hardtops started at $4194. **2.** Three long projections on the front fenders took the place of portholes on '64 Wildcats like this four-door hardtop. **3.** The '64 LeSabre Estate Wagon would be the last big Buick wagon until 1970. **4.** An airy raised roof section made this Buick Skylark Sports Wagon and the related Oldsmobile Vista-Cruiser the talk of station wagon shoppers in '64. Four overhead windows let added light into the cabin; special tinting cut down on glare and heat. **5.** The Special/Skylark line grew from compact to midsize proportions for '64. Wheelbase was up three inches, to 115, and handsome new bodies were 11.4 inches longer than before, at 203.5. The $2834 Skylark ragtop drew 10,225 sales.

THE FIRST TIME YOU CROSS TOWN IN A 1964 CADILLAC

. . . you're going to be amazed at the wonderful way it moves and handles. For this great new car introduces a standard of performance and action that is new even to Cadillac. It comes from an advanced high-performance engine—the most powerful in Cadillac history. It comes from an improved Hydra-Matic Drive—and on some models, a new Turbo Hydra-Matic—that provides incredible response and agility. And it comes from a host of other Cadillac advancements—refined Cadillac power steering, an exclusive true-center drive line, and motordom's only real triple braking system. It's more tempting than ever—and just wait till you drive it! Your dealer will arrange it all.

1. Except for revised badging and detail trim, the Buick Riviera's appearance was unchanged for its second season. Underhood, a 425-cid V-8 replaced the 401 as the standard engine. It made 340 horsepower with the four-barrel carb, or 360 with the optional dual four-barrel setup. **2.** Cadillac's once-soaring tailfins were down to modest blades for 1964—which made the cars look even longer and lower. **3.** The stately Fleetwood Series 60 Special four-door hardtop started at $6388. **4.** Cadillac's most prestigious two-door, the $6630 Eldorado convertible, could be identified by its full rear-wheel cutouts sans fender skirts—the only '64 so styled.

1. GM's answer to Ford's successful Fairlane was the Chevelle, Chevrolet's first midsize car. The top-line Malibu series arrived with a snazzy SS option for the Sport Coupe (shown) and convertible. **2.** Non SS Malibu ragtops started at $2695 with base 283-cid V-8. **3.** Chevy resurrected the El Camino on its new midsize platform. Buyers had a choice of six-cylinder or V-8 power and standard or Custom trim. **4.** Chevy II sales sank for '64, likely "cannibalized" by the new Chevelle. An entry-level 100 two-door sedan started at $2070 with six-cylinder power. **5.** The Monza convertible was a popular Corvair, with sales reaching 31,045.

1. The first Sting Rays earned a reputation as excellent handling and driving machines. A one-piece rear window was the Corvette coupe's big style change for 1964. 2. New wheelcovers and less brightwork also marked '64 Sting Rays. Convertibles again out-sold coupes, 13,925 to 8304. 3. The Grand Sport was an all-out Sting Ray intended for production racing classes, but technical problems and other factors intervened so that only five were built. Private owners raced them through 1966. 4. The big "Jet Smooth" Chevys returned for '64 with a more rounded look on the new-for-'63 bodyshells. Impala Sport Coupes started at $2786. 5. The Biscayne two-door sedan was Chevy's cheapest and lightest big car. This innocent-looking example packs a 409.

'64 Corvette Sting Ray

1

3

2

1. Slightly more conservative styling was the 1964 direction for full-sized Oldsmobiles. Jetstar 88 was introduced as a new economy line below the Dynamic 88 series. With bucket seats, standard 345-hp V-8, and a $3603 price tag, the Jetstar I (shown) was the sportiest and priciest model of this new entry level series. **2.** The second most expensive model in the Jetstar 88 line was the $3318 convertible. This one's chrome wheels are nonstock items. **3.** Ninety-Eight continued as Oldsmobile's flagship line. The $4468 convertible was the series' rarest model, with a production run of just 4004 units. Olds's 330-hp "Skyrocket" 394-cid V-8 was standard in Ninety-Eights and Super 88s. **4.** The F-85 ascended to GM's new 115-inch wheelbase and got a new performance-oriented 4-4-2 package. The name stood for four-barrel carb, four-speed manual gearbox, dual exhausts. A 310-hp 330-cid V-8 was included.

OLDSMOBILE FOR '64
WHERE THE ACTION IS!

NINETY-EIGHT · STARFIRE · SUPER 88 · DYNAMIC 88 · JETSTAR I · JETSTAR 88 · F-85

4

1-2. By stuffing its big 389-cube V-8 into its midsize Tempest, Pontiac created the first modern muscle car, the legendary GTO. Three body styles were offered: the $3500 convertible, $3250 two-door hardtop, and $3200 pillared coupe. GTO's magic was that it was the first "factory hot rod" marketed as an integrated performance package, with a key component being a carefully cultivated image. But it had the goods, too, starting at 325 horsepower with the standard four-barrel carb or 348 with the optional Tri-Power setup. **3.** Big Pontiacs, like the $3578 Bonneville ragtop, got a handsome freshening. A 20-percent jump in overall production helped Pontiac strengthen its hold on third place in the industry.

SCORECARD 1964		
MAKE	TOTAL PRODUCTION	MKT POSITION
BUICK	510,490 ▲	5th ▲
CADILLAC	165,909 ▲	10th •
CHEVROLET	2,318,619 ▲	1st •
OLDSMOBILE	493,991 ▲	7th ▼
PONTIAC	715,261 ▲	3rd •

GENERAL MOTORS

1. GM restyled all its full-sized cars for 1965. Buicks fared well, gaining curvier lines without losing the brand's conservative, upscale elegance. Wildcat's style leader was the $3727 ragtop. *2.* Midsized Buicks got a subtle facelift for '65. Skylark Sportwagons (left) rode a 120-inch wheelbase, five inches longer than their Special siblings (right). *3.* Electra 225 models retained their more stately profile in the '65 redo, as this $4296 hardtop sedan exhibits. *4.* Showing slightly swoopier lines is this $3346 Wildcat four-door sedan. *5.* Skylark, the upscale version of the Special intermediate, became a series of its own and cost about $200 more than comparable Special models. Here, the $2834 Skylark convertible. *6.* Buick joined the blossoming muscle car trend in its own classy way with a performance version of the Skylark called Gran Sport. A 325-hp 401 was part of the option package.

1-2. Buick's Riviera looked better than ever for '65, with headlights newly concealed behind "clamshell" doors flanking the grille. Taillights were relocated to the bumper. A new Gran Sport package included special trim, firmer suspension, styled steel wheels, and a 360-hp "Wildcat" 425 V-8. **3.** Cadillac sales zoomed to nearly 200,000 for a banner 1965. Yet another redesign produced the trimmest Caddys in many a year, highlighted by stacked headlamps and gently curved side windows. Standard Cadillacs rode a 129.5-inch wheelbase, but the extra-posh Fleetwood Sixty Special four-door sedan mounted an exclusive 133-inch span. **4-5.** The ever-popular Coupe DeVille racked up 43,345 sales. Prices started at $5419.

1-2. Though still on a 119-inch wheelbase, Chevrolet's big '65s were longer, wider, and roomier overall, enhanced by a fulsome, flowing new shape. Impala Super Sport production jumped to 243,114 units, again split between Sport Coupes and convertibles like this one. Full-size SS sales would never be so high again. Neither would V-8 options, which again included 283- and 327-cubic-inch small blocks, plus an all-new 396, which replaced the veteran 409 in February 1965. For the big-car line, the new big-block came with four-barrel carburetors to produce 325, 375, or 425 horsepower, the last mainly for racing. "Super Sport" name script replaced SS badges for '65. V-8 Impalas totaled some 746,800 against 56,600 six-cylinder models–no surprise in those days of cheap gas and affordable horsepower. **3.** Again trying the "luxury Impala" idea, Chevy added a $200 Caprice option for the Impala Sport Sedan at mid '65. Included were a lush interior, special trim, and a heavy-duty frame.

1

2

Consider an automobile that has the look of hand-rubbed walnut trim on every door; that seats you on deeply tufted fabric and has deep-twist carpeting underfoot; that relaxes you with a bolster center armrest; that cushions and quiets your ride with extra soundproofing, a heavier frame, a stronger body and a softer suspension . . . that is a Chevrolet Impala luxury option so it won't cost you a king's ransom.
Consider it done.

INTRODUCING THE CAPRICE CUSTOM SEDAN BY CHEVROLET

Caprice CHEVROLET

3

1. The V-8-only Caprice would soon usurp the Impala's top of the line status. **2-3.** Chevy II again saw only detail changes for '65, but a 195-hp 283 V-8 option returned from '64 along with new 250- and 300-hp 327s. Most went into Novas like these SS Sport Coupes, of which 9100 were built. **4-5.** Chevelle got the usual cosmetic changes for '65. Malibu SS was again the top series, available in coupe or convertible body styles with six-cylinder or V-8 power. **6-8.** The sporty Corvair was redesigned for '65 to be a much safer car at any speed. Styled largely by Ron Hill, the new Corvair embodied GM design chief Bill Mitchell's fondness for graceful curves and swells. Both coupes and sedans became pillarless body styles. Pictured here (from left to right) is the complete Monza lineup: the $2347 hardtop coupe, $2422 hardtop sedan, and $2493 convertible.

1. Further refinements marked the '65 Sting Rays. Immediately apparent were the new trio of functional air vents in the front fenders, a smoothed-out hood, and more-legible instruments. Corvette set another sales record for '65 at 23,572; 8186 were coupes. **2.** Standard side exhaust pipes marked Corvettes with the new big-block 396 option. Small-block V-8 power was unchanged, but all Corvettes got standard disc brakes to more effectively rein in their muscle. **3.** A wood-rim steering wheel and telescopic steering column were among several new 'Vette options. The convertible's base price now stood at $4106. **4-5.** After a season of 330-cid propulsion, Oldsmobile's 4-4-2 option moved up to 400 cubes. So 4-4-2 now meant 400 cubic inches, four-barrel carb, and dual exhausts. Though not the lightest or fastest of the breed, the 4-4-2 was plenty quick at around 7.5 seconds 0-60 mph. It was surprisingly agile, too.

1. *Cutlass was the top trim level for the subtly facelifted 1965 Oldsmobile intermediates, and the king Cutlass was the $2983 convertible.* 2. *Full-sized Oldsmobiles adopted curvier lines with "hop-up" rear fenders. The showy Starfire convertible was again the most expensive Olds, starting at $4778. Just 2236 were built.* 3. *Ninety-Eights adapted well to Oldsmobile's new design motif while retaining their unique styling features. Pictured here is the $4197 Holiday sports coupe, one of 12,166 built.* 4-5. *Pontiac GTOs got vertical headlights and other styling updates for '65. The Tri-Power 389 gained 12 horsepower, to 360. While other manufacturers were still hustling to get true muscle cars to market, the GTO had already become a bona-fide pop culture phenomenon. Sales more than doubled, to 75,352.*

1-2. Big Pontiacs added inches and pounds for 1965, but hid their bulk nicely with new, flowing body lines. Shown here are the $3357 coupe and $3594 convertible, which saw production runs of 44,030 and 21,050, respectively. Full-length rocker panel trim accentuated the voluptuous "Coke bottle" countours. **3.** Top-line Bonneville luxury was available to wagon buyers in the six-seat Custom Safari. The $3632 wagon was the least popular Bonneville, with 6460 sold. **4.** Grand Prixs could be distinguished by their vertical-bar grille, full-width taillight, and unique roofline. Prices started at $3498, down $1 from 1964. **5.** A $244 "2+2" option package endowed Catalina coupes or convertibles with special trim, bucket seats, heavy-duty suspension, and a standard 338-hp 421 V-8. Optional were 356- or 376-hp 421s. Pontiac's 10-millionth car–a gold Catalina–rolled off the assembly line in Pontiac, Michigan, this year.

SCORECARD 1965

MAKE	TOTAL PRODUCTION	MKT POSITION
BUICK	600,145 ▲	5th ●
CADILLAC	182,435 ▲	11th ▼
CHEVROLET	2,375,118 ▲	1st ●
OLDSMOBILE	591,701 ▲	6th ▲
PONTIAC	802,000 ▲	3rd ●

1-2. *The Buick Riviera was redesigned for 1966 as an underskin cousin of Oldsmobile's new front-wheel-drive Toronado. Buick, however, stuck with rear-wheel drive. Parking lights were canted in at the leading edges of the front fenders; dual headlights flipped down from above the grille. Two versions of Buick's 425-cid V-8 were offered: one with a single four-barrel carb and 340 horsepower, the other with twin quads and 360 hp.* **3-5.** *A total restyling of all four General Motors intermediate car lines was ordained for '66. Like its corporate siblings, the Skylark Gran Sport was new all over. Buick signaled its commitment to the muscle car market by elevating the Gran Sport from a Skylark option package to its own series of two-door sedans, hardtops, and convertibles. Its 325-hp 401 V-8 delivered 0-60 mph in 7.6 seconds; a quicker 340-hp version was optional.* **6.** *Buick Sportwagons got more power for '66 via a new 340-cid V-8 with 220 or 260 horsepower.*

1

2

3

4

5

6

1. Full-sized Buicks got no drastic change for 1966. Still, engineering tweaks improved quietness and ride comfort a bit, so that year's new "tuned car" ad slogan wasn't all hype. Outside of the Riviera, the Electra 225 convertible was the priciest Buick at $4378. 2-3. Updated trim kept the '66 Wildcats as handsome as ever. A 325-hp 401 was standard. Here, a coupe in Shadow Turquoise. 4-5. The '66 Cadillacs reprised the successful '65 formula, albeit with minor tweaks and two new options: variable-ratio power steering for sportier handling, and heated front seats—another industry first. The $5581 DeVille hardtop sedan accounted for 60,550 sales. 6. The Eldorado retained its exclusive status for '66. Just 2250 of the $6631 ragtops were called for, though that was up slightly from '65.

1. Chevy's new 427-cubic-inch big-block V-8 replaced the 396 as Corvette's top 1966 power option, offering 390 or 425 horsepower. Model-year production set another record with 17,762 ragtops and 9958 coupes like this. The Sting Ray's grille switched from thin horizontal bars to a crosshatch pattern, one of only a handful of subtle appearance changes. 2. Corvette convertibles started at $4084, just over $200 less than their coupe counterparts. To the dismay of many 'Vette lovers, 1966 would be the last year for the factory's optional "knock-off" aluminum wheels. 3. This '66 Corvair Monza convertible is one of 10,345 built; the turbocharged Corsa version saw a mere 3142 copies. Monzas again offered 95 standard hp and 110- and 140-hp options, all from the same 164-cid six. 4. Budget-conscious compact shoppers looked to the Chevy II 100 series, which offered four-door sedans with four-cylinder, six-cylinder, or V-8 power. V-8 models like this one started at $2234.

1

2

3

4

5

6

1-2. The 1966 Chevrolet Caprice was now a separate series comprising two- and four-door hardtops and a four-door wagon. The Custom Coupe came in for special attention due to its formal, thick-pillar roofline, which wasn't shared with any other Chevrolet. **3-4.** Potent midsized muscle cars were all the rage by '66, and the Chevy Chevelle SS 396 was one of the best. Besides clean new looks, a sporty bucket-seat interior, and a fortified chassis, Chevelle's hottest hardtop and convertible packed a standard 396 big-block V-8 with a rousing 325 horses, with up to 375 optional. **5-6.** By its third year, the Olds 4-4-2 had become the benchmark for balanced muscle car performance. No rival handled or stopped better, and with up to 360 hp and factory-available forced air induction, few could ignore it in a straight line. **7-8.** A landmark automobile and one of the decade's most important cars, the 1966 Oldsmobile Toronado reintroduced front-wheel drive to America and forecast the design revolution that would sweep the U.S. industry in the 1980s. Toronado's groundbreaking styling bore hints of the classic 1936-1937 Cord 810/812. **9-10.** Olds' Starfire lost its convertible model for '66, leaving only a $3564 hardtop coupe. Sales reached 13,019. **11.** The $3588 convertible was the priciest and rarest model in Olds' Delta 88 line.

1-2. Pontiac's GTO was promoted into its own model line for 1966 and saw a production run of 96,946 units, the highest-ever total for a true muscle car. Redesigned bodies had a handsome "Coke-bottle" shape. Pillared coupes, hardtops, and convertibles were still offered, again with a 389-cubic-inch V-8; 360-horsepower versions did 0-60 mph in 6.5 seconds. **3.** This year's slightly revised styling looked good on the 124-inch chassis of the Bonneville and Star Chief. Lower-body trim on Bonnevilles got a ribbed texture for '66. Demand for the $3586 Bonneville convertible dipped to 16,299. **4.** Pontiac's entry in the growing personal-luxury field continued to be the Grand Prix hardtop coupe, which was built on the Catalina chassis but featured distinct grille, roof, and rear styling. Pontiac celebrated its 40th birthday in 1966, and built its 11-millionth car in June.

SCORECARD 1966

MAKE	TOTAL PRODUCTION	MKT POSITION
BUICK	553,870 ▼	7th ▼
CADILLAC	196,685 ▲	11th •
CHEVROLET	2,212,415 ▼	1st •
OLDSMOBILE	578,385 ▼	6th •
PONTIAC	831,331 ▲	3rd •

1. Rivieras saw little change on the outside for 1967, but got a new 360-horsepower 430 V-8 under the hood. Sales improved to 42,799. 2. LeSabre continued as Buick's entry-level full-size series, offering standard and Custom trim levels. Shown here is the $3172 Custom hardtop coupe. 3. The Gran Sport lineup got a new "junior" muscle car in the GS340. Available only in white or silver, both with red accents, the GS340 packed a 260-hp 340 V-8. 4. Three-seat Sportwagons started at $3173. The roof rack and chrome wheels seen on this example were extra-cost options. 5. Full-sized Buicks had a new look for '67, highlighted by flowing "sweep-spear" bodyside lines, a nod to 1950s Buick styling. The Electra 225 line saw sales rise by about 12,000 units, to 100,304. Pictured here is the standard two-door hardtop, which listed for $4075.

1-2. Cadillac reserved the Eldorado name for a special car, and that surely described the totally new two-door hardtop that bore the badge for 1967. Adopting the Olds Toronado's front-wheel-drive technology, Caddy fashioned a creased coupe on a 120-inch wheelbase (nine inches briefer than the rear-drive '66 Eldo and one inch less than Toronado). The $6277 Cadillac rode and handled better than the $4850 Olds, and its sales of 17,930 were just 4000 short of Toronado's. Like all '67 Caddys, the Eldo used a 340-hp 429-cid V-8. Many regard the 1967 Eldorado design as one of Cadillac's all-time best. **3.** Cadillac's entry-level Calais series shared bodies with DeVilles, but made do with less-fancy fabrics, and manually adjustable seats and windows. The $5040 Calais two-door hardtop was the cheapest 1967 Cadillac.

1-2. Though overshadowed by the reborn Eldorado, Cadillac's mainstream '67s offered fresh styling highlighted by a forward-raked grille and front fenders. Inside were a new-look dashboard and extra standard features like a tilt-telescope steering wheel and cruise control. The $5608 DeVille convertible was now Cadillac's only ragtop. **3.** The '67 Chevelles sported a crisp facelift. Power-bulge hood vents on SS396s looked great, but weren't functional. This $3033 SS396 ragtop was one of 63,000 SS Chevelles built for the model year. **4.** A "tunnelback" roofline carried over for '67 on Chevelle Sport Coupes, including the muscular SS396, which priced from $2825. Super Sports cost about $285 more than comparable Malibu models. **5-6.** Novas sported just minor trim changes for '67. Most coupes got six-cylinder power (left), but SSs (right) could be equipped with a potent 350-horsepower 327 V-8.

1

2

3

1-2. Chevrolet's Mustang-fighting Camaro debuted for 1967. The Z-28 package was created for the Sports Car Club of America's year-old Trans-American race series for compact "sedans." Broad dorsal stripes, "Rally" wheels on red-line tires, uprated F41 suspension, and a high-winding 302-cubic-inch small-block V-8 were included in the option, which was available only for the hardtop Sport Coupe at about $3800 delivered. Just 602 were built for '67 and have long been among the most prized of early Camaros. **3.** Camaro didn't bother with a fastback like Mustang, but wore its own very clean styling in the curvy, contemporary GM mold. This convertible priced from $2704 with 230-cid six, $2809 with base 210-hp 327 V-8.

4

5

4. The "Command Performance" Camaro was extolled in this early ad as "Chevrolet's new driving machine with big-car stability and big-car power." Actually, it was the bow-tie answer to Ford's phenomenally successful 1965-66 Mustang ponycar. Camaro's dashboard was a reverse-slant design similar to Corvair's; a tachometer and full engine gauges were part of a mile-long options list. **5.** Hidden headlamps identified Camaros equipped with the Rally Sport appearance package, which could be combined with the performance-oriented SS option. Grille sections at each end powered aside to uncover the headlamps. SS goodies included stiffer springs and shocks, Firestone Wide Oval tires, performance hood, and "bumble-bee" nose stripes.

1-2. Still regarded by many as one of the best 'Vettes of all time, the '67 Sting Ray got five smaller front fender vents, new rocker panel trim, and slotted Rally wheels. Ironically, year-to-year sales eased for the first time in years, slipping to 22,940 units. **3.** Keeping to a two-year design cycle, full-sized 1967 Chevys got brand-new bodyshells with flowing lines that made the cars appear longer, though overall length and wheelbase were unchanged. Top-performing Impalas were the rare SS427-equipped coupes (shown) and convertibles. **4.** The Biscayne two-door sedan remained the most affordable big Chevy for '67, starting at $2442 with standard 230-cubic-inch six. **5-6.** The Oldsmobile F-85/Cutlass line saw a modest facelift. Gutsy 4-4-2 models, like this $3118 convertible, packed a 350-horsepower 400-cubic-inch V-8.

1. Full-sized Oldsmobiles got curvier for 1967, and were again led by the Ninety-Eight series. Here, the $4498 Ninety-Eight convertible. **2.** The most popular member of Olds' midpriced Delta 88 lineup was the $3328 Holiday hardtop sedan, with 33,326 produced. **3-4.** Olds Toronados were updated with freshened front-end styling and new taillights. Toronado shared with all big Oldsmobiles a 425-cid V-8, though it had 385 hp to the others' 300-375. **5.** Pontiac Grand Prixs stood apart from their Catalina kin with a hidden-headlamp nose and unique tail. A Grand Prix convertible was a 1967-only offering. **6.** Pontiac Bonneville hardtop sedans started at $3517. **7.** Pontiac's midline full-sized cars were renamed Executives for '67, losing their Star Chief monikers. The $3165 four-door sedan was the line's best-seller.

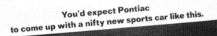

1-2. Pontiac's big news for 1967 was the introduction of the Firebird "ponycar." Though based on Chevrolet's new Camaro, Firebird had Pontiac engines and styling cues, plus slightly more-upscale trim and pricing. Like Camaro, coupes and convertibles were offered, starting at $2666 and $2903, respectively. Engines were a 230-cubic-inch six-cylinder and V-8s of 326 and 400 cid. Pontiac's pony cost about $200 more than comparable Camaros, and its model-year production of 82,560 paled next to the 220,900 Camaros built. **3-4.** GTOs got minor styling updates such as a mesh grille and resculpted tail, and a 400-cid V-8 replaced the 389. Hardtop coupes like this one started at $2935. A $263 Ram Air package included hardware that opened the otherwise nonfunctional hood scoops. Of 782,734 Pontiacs built for '67, nearly 82,000 were GTOs.

SCORECARD 1967		
MAKE	TOTAL PRODUCTION	MKT POSITION
BUICK	562,507 ▲	5th ▲
CADILLAC	200,000 ▲	11th ●
CHEVROLET	1,948,410 ▼	1st ●
OLDSMOBILE	548,390 ▼	6th ●
PONTIAC	782,734 ▼	3rd ●

1-2. As with other GM intermediates, midsized Buicks gained an inch of wheelbase and far more rounded sheet-metal for 1968. Gran Sports became a separate series, but still shared their hardtop coupe and convertible bodies with Skylarks. Shown here is the $2926 GS350, Buick's "junior" Gran Sport, which was powered by a 280-horsepower 350-cubic-inch V-8. Big-brother GS400 models got a 340-hp 400. **3.** Buick sold the flashy glass-roof Sportwagon as a separate model in six-passenger form for $3341, or with seating for nine for $158 more. Pseudo-wood trim was optional. **4.** Buicks were a step down from their Cadillac cousins in terms of absolute automotive luxury, but carried almost as much prestige. Buick's most popular '68 model, with sales of 50,846 units, was the $4509 Electra 225 Custom four-door hardtop. **5.** Midline Wildcat four-door sedans started at a less luxurious $3416. **6.** Riviera got a more massive look for '68 via a restyled nose and tail. Sales were up slightly, to 49,284.

1. Air-pollution laws took effect for 1968, and Cadillac was ready with a new 472-cubic-inch V-8. It ran cleaner than the 429 it replaced, and delivered 35 more horsepower, a rousing 375 in all. Sales were down a bit for the model year, but still quite healthy. **2.** Senior Cadillacs sported new grilles and, thanks to longer hoods, hidden windshield wipers. The demise of the Lincoln Continental four-door convertible left Cadillac and Imperial with the only soft tops among American luxury cars. By '68, the starting price of a DeVille convertible (shown) was up to $5736. **3-4.** Government-mandated side-marker lights were among the few visual changes for Eldorados.

1-2. The 1968 Corvette wore a swoopy new body atop the 1963-67 chassis, and dispensed with the Sting Ray name. Though the styling was controversial at the time, Corvette production rose to 28,566, a new all-time high. **3.** Full-sized '68 Chevys wore a nice update of their '67 styling. Here, the Impala wagon, which started at $3245. **4.** Reflecting the waning interest in sporty big cars, the Impala Super Sport returned to option status for '68. The package cost $179. **5.** Camaro wasn't altered much for its sophomore year, but optional four-wheel disc brakes arrived midyear and were especially welcome on high-power models like this Z-28. **6-7.** Chevelles were built on GM's all-new midsize platform for '68. Shown here, the SS396 coupe and the Malibu hardtop sedan.

1. Chevy II went to almost intermediate size for 1968 with a full redesign on a new 111-inch wheelbase that owed much to Chevelle. Models were cut to just two- and four-door sedans. **2.** Oldsmobile teamed with aftermarket shifter manufacturer Hurst to produce the limited-edition Hurst/Olds. It packed a 390-hp 455 Toronado V-8. **3-4.** The '68 Vista Cruiser, like other Olds intermediates, got an updated version of the "barbell" grille design that had been used on midsized Oldsmobiles since 1965. **5.** The powerhouse 4-4-2's 400-cid V-8 made 350 hp, or 360 with optional W-30 hop-ups. Priciest of the lineup was the $3341 convertible.

Once you've tried Wide-Tracking in a LeMans you'll understand why we call it LeMans.

Wide-Track **68** Pontiacs

1. Pontiac's 1968 intermediate models wore curvaceous new styling on GM's new 112-inch-wheelbase chassis. The $2839 Tempest Custom convertible was the most affordable droptop in the line. **2.** As before, LeMans was a step up the model roster from Tempest. Engine choices for these midline midsized cars ranged from a 175-hp 215-cid six to a 320-hp 350 V-8. **3-4.** GTOs wore a handsome new Endura front bumper, a dent-resistant plastic unit color-matched to the body. Hidden headlights were an extremely popular option. A 400-cubic-inch V-8, now at 350 horsepower, was standard, with 265- and 360-hp versions optional. The last did 0-60 mph in 6.4 seconds. GTO sales rose by about 6000 units, to 87,684. The $3101 hardtop accounted for 77,704; the $3227 convertible made up the balance.

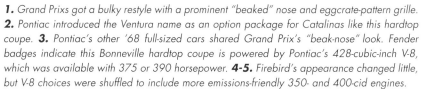

1. Grand Prixs got a bulky restyle with a prominent "beaked" nose and eggcrate-pattern grille. **2.** Pontiac introduced the Ventura name as an option package for Catalinas like this hardtop coupe. **3.** Pontiac's other '68 full-sized cars shared Grand Prix's "beak-nose" look. Fender badges indicate this Bonneville hardtop coupe is powered by Pontiac's 428-cubic-inch V-8, which was available with 375 or 390 horsepower. **4-5.** Firebird's appearance changed little, but V-8 choices were shuffled to include more emissions-friendly 350- and 400-cid engines.

SCORECARD 1968		
MAKE	TOTAL PRODUCTION	MKT POSITION
BUICK	651,823 ▲	5th ●
CADILLAC	230,003 ▲	11th ●
CHEVROLET	2,139,290 ▲	1st ●
OLDSMOBILE	562,459 ▲	7th ▼
PONTIAC	910,977 ▲	3rd ●

1. Buick's midsized models returned with few changes for 1969, though GS400s got functional hood scoops. This GS400 convertible is fitted with the optional Stage 1 package, which boosted the 400-cubic-inch V-8 from 340 horsepower to 345–on paper. The actual increase was probably more. 2. New bodies with new variations on similar styling themes marked Buick's full-sized cars for '69. This Electra 225 Custom four-door hardtop wears the Limited option package, which included special trim and a vinyl top. 3. Buick Wildcats, formerly based on the larger Electra 225, were now sportier versions of the smaller LeSabre but still carried the Electra's 360-hp 430 V-8. A Custom two-door hardtop went for $3917, about $430 more than a comparable LeSabre. 4. Buick's dome-top Sportwagon models made their final appearance in 1969. 5. Rivieras didn't change much, but sold better than ever, with a production run of nearly 53,000 units. 6-7. Ventless door glass and bladelike front fenders were new elements of Cadillac's new look for 1969. Accessory wire wheels dress up this DeVille convertible. 8. The '69 Eldorado sported a fresh face with exposed headlamps, but Cadillac's modern classic was otherwise little-changed.

1. Recontoured below-the-belt sheetmetal with racy rear fender "speed-lines" gave a huskier, more "performance" look to all '69 Camaros. This Z/28 wears the $179 RS package, which included unique retractable headlight covers. **2.** This unassuming Camaro is one of just 69 produced with the all-aluminum ZL1 427 V-8, one of Chevy's most exotic and powerful engines. **3.** This Camaro convertible was one of 17,573 built for the model year. Camaro would then do without a ragtop for the next 17 years. **4.** In a move that surprised no one, Chevy ended Corvair production on May 14, 1969, after five years of controversy and falling sales. Exactly 6000 of the '69s were built, again divided among "500" and Monza coupes and this $2641 Monza convertible, one of a final 521.

1-2. The '69 Corvettes revived the Stingray name and set another sales record with a production run of 38,762. Coupes outsold ragtops for the first time. This coupe packs the mighty 435-hp, triple-carb 427. **3.** The two-year-old styling of the full-sized Chevys was handsomely updated for '69, announced by a broad loop-style bumper/grille. The Impala Super Sport made one final stand as a $422 package for the two-door hardtop (shown) and convertible. **4.** Top-line big-Chevy wagon was the Kingswood Estate, trimmed to Caprice level and identified by woody-look side trim. **5.** Chevelle's year-old styling was just mildly tweaked for '69. Malibu Sport Coupes priced from $2690 with base 307 V-8. **6.** The Chevy II name was retired for '69 in favor of Nova.

1-2. Oldsmobile's Cutlass lineup got a modest facelift for 1969, and was again keynoted by the sporty 4-4-2, which started at $3395 in convertible form. All 4-4-2s had a wacky pitchman in the fictional Dr. Oldsmobile, the mustachioed, white-lab-coat-wearing "mad scientist" of Olds performance. **3-4.** Though redesigned on a one-inch-longer wheelbase, the full-size Delta 88 didn't look much different than before. The convertible moved from the departed Delmont 88 series to become a $3590 Delta 88. Base engine was a 250-hp 350 V-8; options ranged to a 390-hp 455. **5.** Toronado, still Oldsmobile's only front-wheel-drive car, saw little change for 1969 after its '68 facelift. Offered as a base and Custom hardtop coupe, it had a 375-hp or optional 400-hp 455 V-8. Prices started at $4835.

The more we hide, the more you see. That's a Break Away!

Seems like a lot of "elegant" cars end up looking like ads for The Shiny-Brite Chrome Works.

Pontiac has nothing against Shiny-Brite, you understand. We simply don't do things that way. Quite the opposite. As the 1969 Grand Prix below illustrates. Grand Prix's disappearing act started last year with the windshield wipers. Owners liked them so much, we put our clever engineers back to work. They managed to make a 10-foot radio antenna vanish into thin air.

The door handles aren't quite as baffling. But they are recessed to keep the lines clean.

Vent windows? Gone the way of the dodo. Who needs them? Pontiac's upper-level ventilation provides the air without the wind noise.

Here comes the irony. With all that's invisible, Grand Prix's styling is undoubtedly the most noticed (and liked) on the road. Even the chrome buffs are starting to break away.

Break Away in a **⩔** Wide-Track Grand Prix

1-2. Bucking an industry trend, the redesigned 1969 Grand Prix shrunk three inches in wheelbase (to 118 inches) and lost 360 pounds (now 3715). Yet the trimmer GP sported one of the longest hoods in autodom, and with V-8s up to a 390-horsepower 428 available, it combined muscle car go with luxury-car comfort. **3-4, 6.** "The Great One" got minor styling updates and a whimsical new performance model for '69. Pontiac added op-art decals, a rear spoiler, and a 366-hp Ram Air III 400 to create The Judge, a $332 option package on the GTO. **5.** Like the GTO, Tempest and LeMans models saw modest trim updates. This LeMans ragtop sports the optional hood-mounted tachometer. **7, 10.** Even considering its midyear debut, first-year production of the legendary Trans Am was minuscule at only 697 units, including just eight convertibles. Included in the $725 Trans Am option package was the 366-hp Ram Air 400 and heavy-duty suspension. All were painted Polar White with blue racing stripes. **8-9.** Pontiac's full-sized cars were redesigned, but looked very similar to the '68s. Catalinas rode a 122-inch wheelbase, while Executives and Bonnevilles had a 125-inch span—both one inch longer than before. Catalina ragtops started at $3476.

5

7

6

8

9

10

SCORECARD 1969		
MAKE	TOTAL PRODUCTION	MKT POSITION
BUICK	635,422 ▼	5th ●
CADILLAC	223,237 ▼	11th ●
CHEVROLET	2,092,947 ▼	1st ●
OLDSMOBILE	635,241 ▲	6th ▲
PONTIAC	870,081 ▼	3rd ●

STUDEBAKER

America's oldest maker of wheeled vehicles abandoned the auto business in 1966 after a decade marked by too many setbacks and too few successes. Studebaker started way back in 1852 building horse-drawn wagons, including the covered Conestoga rigs that carried settlers to the Wild West. The company prospered anew with horseless carriages starting in 1902, establishing a solid reputation while outlasting hundreds of other independent carmakers. After surviving a near-death experience in the early Depression years, Studebaker roared back to health with the stylish, low-priced 1939 Champion. In 1947, it surprised everyone in being "First by Far With a Postwar Car," another head-turning success from famed industrial designer Raymond Loewy. Three years later, the company's South Bend plant turned out a record 343,000 cars. By 1952, Studebaker had a modern, lively V-8 and ambitious plans for its second century.

Trouble was, a cutthroat Big Three price war was killing the much smaller independents, which lacked the resources to compete. So although Studebaker managed a fleet of all-new Loewy-designed 1953 models, its sales and profits kept sliding. With bulking up looming as imperative for survival, Studebaker agreed to be bought by luxury legend Packard as a first step toward a grand alliance with fellow independents Nash and Hudson. That plan fell through, however, and Studebaker-Packard was on the ropes by 1958. Desperate for cash, S-P managers secured a takeover by aircraft maker Curtiss-Wright, which promptly dumped Packard and bet everything on a compact Studebaker. Though the resulting 1959 Lark was just a cutdown, restyled '53, it was a perfectly timed hit. Studebaker was saved.

But only for the moment. Popular though it was, the Lark didn't bring in enough cash to fund more salable new products, and the Big Three upped the pressure for 1960 by introducing compacts of their own. As a result, Studebaker could do little more than keep updating the Lark and related Hawk "family sports car," another legacy of 1953. Sales began sinking toward oblivion.

Hope briefly flickered after hard-charging Sherwood Egbert took over as president of Studebaker Corporation in 1961. While designer Brooks Stevens kept working minor miracles freshening the old stuff, Egbert called on Loewy to create a knockout sports coupe that would convince an increasingly doubtful public that Studebaker had a future. Despite little time or money, a talented team quickly produced the Avanti, one of the most memorable cars of the decade. By the time it arrived, however, Studebaker was beyond help. Buyers had lost all confidence in the marque.

Management made a desperate last stand in late 1963, dropping the Avanti and Hawk, closing the century-old South Bend factory, and consolidating production at a small plant in Canada. It didn't work. In the end, Studebaker died from being caught in the sort of vicious downward spiral that would claim another automotive centenarian, Oldsmobile, some 40 years later.

1

2

3

4

5

1-2. *Studebaker added a Lark convertible for 1960, the only ragtop in the compact class. Offered solely in uplevel Regal trim, it started at $2621 with a 90-horsepower 169.6-cubic-inch L-head six or $2756 with Studebaker's veteran 259.2-cid V-8, again rated at 180 hp. The debut 1959 Larks drew over 131,000 sales. Despite a broader lineup, the 1960s slipped two percent to just under 128,000, but that was good going given strong new Big Three competition and a continuing press from American Motors' compact Ramblers.* 3. *Also new for 1960 were four-door Lark wagons on the same 113-inch wheelbase as the two-door versions. A 108.5-inch span again served two- and four-door sedans and hardtop coupes, plus the new convertibles. Wagons priced from $1976 for a Deluxe six-cylinder two-door to $2726 for a V-8 Regal four-door.* 4. *This Lark "Regal VIII" four-door sedan priced from $2331. The "Regal VI" version started at $2196.* 5-6. *The Hawk sports coupe returned for 1960 as one model with a standard 210-horsepower 289-cubic-inch V-8. Base price was $2650. Sales fell by half to 3939 units.*

6

1-2. Basically a restyled version of Studebaker's 1953-55 coupe, the Hawk arrived for 1956 as a four-model line of "family sports cars." The basic design, another effort by the Raymond Loewy team, made a final bow for 1961. Though virtually unchanged, it drew as many sales as the year before. **3-4.** Larks received a subtle restyle for 1961 and added a nicely furnished V-8 Land Cruiser sedan on the longer wagon wheelbase. The big news that year, however, was a modern overhead-valve six to replace an elderly L-head unit. Dubbed "Skybolt Six," it produced 112 horsepower from 169.9 cubic inches. Buyers liked it, snapping up over 41,000 six-cylinder Larks like this Regal ragtop, almost twice the sales of V-8 models. Worrisomely, though, total Lark volume plunged nearly 50 percent to just under 67,000.

1-2. Designer Brooks Stevens had just $7 million to update the entire '62 Studebaker line, yet managed to give Larks new front and rear ends, rooflines, and dashboards; all showing definite European influence. Responding to the sporty-compact craze were a new bucket seat Daytona convertible and hardtop coupe. All this helped Lark sales bounce back to over 93,000 for the model year. **3.** Somehow, Stevens' slim budget also covered a startling makeover of the old Hawk into the clean, modern Grand Turismo Hawk hardtop coupe. Priced from $3095 with standard 210-horsepower 289-cubic-inch V-8, the GT Hawk drew 8388 orders, over double the previous tally. **4.** A novel "Skytop" fabric sunroof was a new $185 option for '62 Lark hardtops and sedans like this Regal Six. **5.** The V-8 Land Cruiser sedan priced from $2493 for '62.

1

2

3

4

5

6

1-2. Seeking a stronger corporate image and a surefire showroom lure, Studebaker turned to Raymond Loewy for a high-style sports coupe. Named Avanti, Italian for "forward," it bowed for 1963 with a curvy fiberglass body atop a Lark chassis. The steep $4495 base price included a 240-horsepower 289-cubic-inch V-8, with a 290-hp supercharged version available. Initial public interest was high, but was fast diluted by workmanship glitches, delivery delays and a new Chevrolet Corvette. As a result, model-year sales were disappointing at 3834. **3-4.** Larks got modest trim changes for '63, as seen on this Daytona convertible and hardtop coupe. **5.** Closed models also received thin-section door frames, as on this "Super Lark" Custom two-door with the newly optional 290-hp "R-2" Avanti engine. **6.** A unique sliding rear roof panel gave sky's-the-limit hauling ability for 1963's new Studebaker Wagonaire models like this top-line Daytona.

1-3. Another Brooks Stevens restyle marked the 1964 Larks, which were now just Studebakers. Models regrouped into Challenger, Commander, and top-line Daytona series priced from $1943 to $2843. The luxury Cruiser sedan and sporty Daytonas had their attractions, but the public was wary, so sales fell to 43,884 from 73,192. **4-5.** Avanti got a few trim tweaks for '64, but retained an aircraft-inspired cockpit with novel glovebox vanity. Despite an unchanged price, sales withered to just 809. **6.** Wagonaires were practical family haulers, but very few were sold for '64, making this Daytona a rare survivor. **7.** Like Avanti, the GT Hawk made a brief appearance for '64. Only 1767 were built.

1-2. In a last-ditch effort to stay in business, Studebaker dropped the Avanti and Hawk, closed its historic South Bend, Indiana, plant, and gamely offered a truncated line of '65 standard cars built in Hamilton, Ontario, Canada. The surviving Commander and Daytona sedans and wagons looked little different from '64, but switched to Chevrolet engines: a 120-horsepower 194-cubic-inch six and 195-hp 283-cid V-8. Daytonas like this $2565 Sport Sedan had the V-8 standard. **3.** Studebaker also dropped fixed-roof wagons for '65, leaving Wagonaires in six- and eight-cylinder Commander trim and this top-line $2890 V-8 Daytona. **4.** The swanky Cruiser sedan also hung on for '65, selling from $2470. For all the penny-pinching, total '65 Studebaker sales came to only 14,435.

1-2. With cash running low and no sales upturn in sight, Studebaker left the auto business on March 17, 1966, after building 8947 lightly facelifted models. Offerings for '66 comprised this Daytona Sport Sedan, two- and four-door Commander sedans, a four-door Wagonaire, and a Cruiser sedan, all available with six or V-8. Prices ran $2060 to $2645. A last new feature was "Refreshaire," a windows-up ventilation system with small air vents at the taillamps. **3.** The '66 Cruiser sedan listed at $2405 with base six, $2545 with V-8. Studebaker had several interesting new-model ideas in the works that might have saved the day had they reached the market. It didn't matter in the end, however, because Studebaker had diversified enough by 1966 that it could go on just fine without making cars–as indeed it did.

SCORECARD 1960-66		
YEAR	TOTAL PRODUCTION	MKT POSITION
1960	120,465 ▼	11th •
1961	59,713 ▼	12th ▼
1962	89,318 ▲	12th •
1963	69,555 ▼	12th •
1964	36,697 ▼	12th •
1965	19,435 ▼	13th ▼
1966	8,947 ▼	14th ▼